# The Visitor's Guide To Knole, In The County Of Kent: With Catalogues Of The Pictures Contained In The Mansion, And Biographical Notices Of The Principal Persons Whose Portraits Form Part Of The Collection...

John Henry Brady (F. R. A. S.), John Henry Brady

THE VISITOR'S

# GUIDE TO KNOLE.

D

# THE VISITOR'S
# GUIDE TO KNOLE,

IN THE COUNTY OF KENT,

WITH

## CATALOGUES OF THE PICTURES

CONTAINED IN THE MANSION,

AND

## BIOGRAPHICAL NOTICES

OF

THE PRINCIPAL PERSONS WHOSE PORTRAITS FORM
PART OF THE COLLECTION.

---

## BY JOHN H. BRADY, F.R.A.S.

---

SEVENOAKS:
PRINTED BY AND FOR JAMES PAYNE.
LONDON:
SOLD BY SIMPKIN & MARSHALL, STATIONERS' COURT,
AND J. R. SMITH, OLD COMPTON STREET.
1839.

ENTERED AT STATIONERS' HALL.

TO

THE RIGHT HONOURABLE

MARY,

COUNTESS-DOWAGER OF PLYMOUTH,

This Volume,

DESCRIPTIVE OF HER LADYSHIP'S RESIDENCE,

WHICH HAS LONG BEEN KNOWN BY THE NAME OF

KNOLE HOUSE,

AND HAS BEEN

FOR SEVERAL GENERATIONS THE SEAT OF THE ANCIENT

FAMILY OF SACKVILLE,

HER LADYSHIP'S PATERNAL ANCESTORS,

IS,

BY HER LADYSHIP'S KIND PERMISSION,

Dedicated,

WITH FEELINGS OF GRATITUDE AND THE GREATEST RESPECT,

BY

HER LADYSHIP'S MOST OBEDIENT

HUMBLE SERVANT,

JAMES PAYNE.

# ADVERTISEMENT.

---

THIS work, which has been undertaken
with the view of affording to persons
visiting this deservedly celebrated mansion
an opportunity of carrying away with them
some memento of its attractions, is now
put forth as a candidate for public appro-
bation; and the publisher trusts that, in
consideration of the great care which has
been taken in its compilation and revision,
the reader will kindly excuse involuntary
faults, or unintentional errors, if any such
should be detected.

The original intention was, to have produced a work not exceeding two shillings and sixpence in price; but materials were so plentiful, that selection for a volume of that size was impracticable, and an advance of one shilling was determined on, at which price subscribers for the small copies will be supplied; this, however, not exceeding the *cost price* per copy of a large edition, a further advance of one shilling, to non-subscribers, has been deemed necessary; and, considering the quantity of information contained in the volume, the number of its illustrations (all of which have some direct allusion, either to the mansion or its possessors), and the execution of the whole, it is believed that the present price will not be thought beyond its value.

It may be proper to mention here, that the work referred to in a note on the seventh page of this volume will not, in all probability, appear before the ensuing summer; of its publication, however, due notice will be given.

In conclusion, the proprietor begs to return his most respectful acknowledgments to the nobility, gentry, and others, for the encouragement they have afforded him by entering their names as subscribers for this work, and he sincerely hopes that their expectations will be fully realized.

*Sevenoaks, July,* 1839.

# PREFACE.

It is matter of common remark, that the most interesting objects lose much of their attraction from the want of information concerning them; and as this deficiency has been for a considerable time felt with respect to Knole House and its fine collection of pictures, it is hoped that the present attempt to remedy it will be received with favour.

The author, by the kind permission of the lady of the mansion, has been indulged with free access, and allowed every opportunity of forming, unobserved and unrestricted, a correct and impartial opinion of the objects described.

Much interesting information has been
communicated by Mr. Wm. Elliott, who
has long been intimately acquainted with
nearly every part of the mansion, and
whose remarks on the architecture of the
building and decorations of the apartments
will be readily discovered from the minute-
ness of detail into which he enters; while
the work has been embellished by the
pencil of Mr. William Knight, whose
faithful delineation of the subjects selected
cannot fail to reflect credit on him as an
artist. In addition to this, the works of
writers whose authenticity is acknowledged,
have been consulted, and, as far as applicable, incorporated: the author, therefore,
believes that his little volume will be found
what it professes to be, a satisfactory
" guide" for the visitor of Knole.

For the numerous biographical notices
which will be found in its pages, he has

been indebted to such various authorities, that it were difficult to acknowledge all his obligations. He must, however, particularly mention " Burnet's History of his own Times," De Grammont's and Walpole's " Memoirs," and Cunningham's " Lives of Eminent Englishmen." This portion of his volume; comprising as it does, many interesting particulars of the actions and characters of a considerable number of the most eminent ecclesiastics, statesmen, and warriors of the sixteenth century, besides others of a later date, including all the principal members of the noble house of Dorset, cannot fail, as the author hopes, to compensate his trouble, by being deemed an acceptable and valuable addition to his work on Knole, where the portraits of these distinguished personages will be seen.

*London, May* 1, 1839.

# CONTENTS.

# LIST OF ENGRAVINGS.

# GUIDE TO KNOLE HOUSE.

Fire-place bearing the cognizance of archbishop Bourchier.

## THE POSSESSORS OF KNOLE.

THE earliest authentic record concerning the occupancy of this place is found in the reign of king John, when the manor and estate of Knole, with those of Braborne, or Bradborne, Kemsing and Seale, were

B

possessed by Baldwin de Bethun, earl of
Albemarle, who, in the fifth year of that
reign, gave them in "frank marriage" with
his daughter Alice, to William Mareschal,
earl of Pembroke, after whose death, his
eldest brother William Mareschal, succeeded
to the earldom and estates; but taking part
with the rebellious barons, at the latter end
of king John's, and the beginning of king
Henry the Third's reign, his lands were
escheated to the crown; during which time,
as Mr. Hasted thinks, these manors were
granted to Falcatius (or Fulk) de Brent, a
soldier of fortune, of mean extraction, who
had come from the Low Countries with some
foreign auxiliaries to king John's assistance,
and found such favour both from that
monarch and his son, Henry III, that he
was invested with considerable power, and
had the lands of many of the barons conferred on him; till, giving loose to his
natural inclination, he became guilty of
great cruelties and oppressions, and at
length having sided with prince Louis of
France, in his design of invading England,
he was banished the realm, and died soon

afterwards in Italy. After this, the earl of Pembroke, returning to his allegiance, obtained possession of his manors again. This earl, as well as his three brothers, died without issue, and the estates devolved on their five sisters and their heirs; in consequence of which, Roger, son of Hugh Bigod, earl of Norfolk, who married Maud, the eldest sister, became entitled, and died seised of these estates about the fifty-fourth year of Henry III, without issue, leaving Roger Bigod, his nephew, his next heir; who, in the eleventh year of king Edward I, conveyed them to Otho de Grandison; who, dying without issue, was succeeded by his brother William de Grandison; and his grandson, Sir Thomas Grandison, according to Philpott, tranferred Knole to Geoffry de Say, and the rest of the estate to other hands.

This Geoffry de Say (only son and heir of Geoffry de Say, by Idonea, daughter of William, and sister and heiress of Thomas Lord Leyborne) was a man of considerable eminence, having been summoned to parliament in the first year of king Edward III, and afterwards constituted admiral of the fleet, being at that time a knight-banneret. After this, he was constantly employed in the wars in France till his death, which happened on the 26th June, in the year 1359, 33rd Edward III. He married Maud, daughter of Guy de Beauchamp, earl of Warwick, by whom he left issue William, his son and heir, and three daughters, which three daughters eventually became co-heiresses to this property, which continued in the family till the reign of Henry VI, when one Ralph Leghe conveyed the whole estate by sale (though how *he* became possessed of it does not appear) to James Fiennes, whose grandmother was the youngest of the three coheiresses before-mentioned.

This gentleman was a soldier who had eminently distinguished himself in the wars with France under Henry V. In the 24th Henry VI, he was, by an especial writ, summoned to parliament as lord Say and Sele; and, in consideration of his eminent services, in open parliament advanced to the dignity of baron of this realm by the title of lord Say. After this, honours came thick upon him : he was appointed constable of Dover Castle, and warden of the Cinque Ports; then lord chamberlain and one of the king's council; and in the 20th Henry VI, lord-treasurer of England. This rapid advancement, at a time of general discontent, excited the ill-will and hatred of the people, to appease which, the king sequestered lord Say from his office of treasurer; and shortly after, on the insurrection under Jack Cade, committed him to the Tower, with the view, as is supposed, of insuring his safety. The rebels, however, entered London, and growing more insolent with the increase of their numbers, they dragged the lord Say from the Tower, and after a kind of mock-trial at the Guildhall, they hurried him to the Standard in Cheapside, where they cut off his head, and carried it on a pole before his naked body, which was dragged at a horse's tail into Southwark, and there drawn and quartered. There is a scene in Shakspeare's Henry VI, illustrative of this tragedy.

Sir William Fiennes, lord Say and Sele,

only son and heir of James, being deeply
concerned in the contentions between the
houses of York and Lancaster, was compelled to sell the greater part of his possessions. Among others, he, by indenture
dated June 30, 34th Henry VI, conveyed to
Thomas Bourchier, archbishop of Canterbury, for 400 marks, his manor of Knole,
with other estates not necessary to be here
specified.

In the "Survey of Kent," by Kilburne
of Hawkherst, it is stated that archbishop
Bourchier "*rebuilt* the manor-house, in-
closed a park round the same, and resided
much at it." At his death, which happened
on the 30th March, 1486, he bequeathed
the manor and its appurtenances to the see
of Canterbury.

Archbishop Moreton, successor of Bourchier in the see, a cardinal of the church of
Rome, and lord-chancellor of England, also
resided here much, during which time he
too is said to have laid out great sums in
repairing and augmenting the house; and
king Henry VII, in his sixth year, appears
to have honoured him with a visit here

more than once. This learned and eminently good prelate died at Knole House,
in October 1500, and was succeeded in the
see of Canterbury by Henry Dene, bishop
of Salisbury, who preferred and mostly resided at the neighbouring palace at Otford.*
His occupancy of the see of Canterbury was
but brief: he died at Lambeth in February
1502, and was succeeded by William Warham, bishop of London, lord chancellor of
England, and chancellor of Oxford.

Archbishop Warham, styled by Erasmus
"a most accomplished and perfect prelate,"
filled the see of Canterbury for thirty years,
during the first twelve of which, at least,
he resided much at Knole, where he was
frequently visited by kings Henry VII and
VIII, between the years 1504 and 1514;
after which, he expended a vast sum in im-
proving the neighbouring palace at Otford,

---

* The author may fairly be excused for here announcing,
that an account of the ancient palace, and its present ruins,
at Otford, will be found in a little volume, written by him
as a companion to the present, descriptive of Sevenoaks,
and the neighbourhood for some miles round, including
Otford, Penshurst Place, Hever Castle, &c.

where he principally resided till his death, which happened in the year 1532.

His successor in the archbishopric was the celebrated Thomas Cranmer,\* who, finding that the vast possessions of the church excited envy and murmurings, resolved on a voluntary surrender of a part, as the best means of preserving the remainder; and accordingly, by indenture dated November 30, anno 29th Henry VIII (still extant in the Augmentation Office) he granted Knole and its appurtenances, with other manors, together of the yearly value of £503. 14s. 5d, to the king and his successors.  During the period which intervened between the death of Warham and the date of this surrender, being about seven years, it is believed that Cranmer resided frequently at Knole house; in one of the rooms of which are five shields of arms of the Cranmer family.  Near this is another apartment, which has some appearance of having been the archbishop's private chapel; the window resembles more that of a place of worship than any other window in the house, and the approach to

---

\* For biographical notice, see Appendix, No. 17.

it is by two or three steps, exhibiting altogether the appearance of what was once an
altar.

Knole House, with its park and other
lands, remained in the hands of the crown
until the fourth year of the reign of king
Edward VI., Sir Richard Long, knt.,
having been appointed keeper thereof, anno
30th Henry VIII, and Sir Robert South-
well, knt., having held the same office, anno
3rd Edward VI. In the succeeding year
(18th July, 4th Edward VI.) the king, by his
letters patent, granted the manor and park
of Knole, with other estates, to John Dudley,
earl of Warwick, his wife, and their heirs,
in exchange for other premises.

The earl of Warwick was at this time
lord-steward of the king's household; in
the ensuing year he was created duke of
Northumberland, constituted earl-marshal
of England, and warden of the marches
towards Scotland; two years after which,
in the seventh year of King Edward VI,
he sold to the king, in exchange for other
lands, his lordship and manor of Knole

(and other premises), reserving, however, to himself and his heirs for ever, Knole-house, its orchards, gardens, out-buildings, &c.

On the death of the protector Somerset, whose ruin he is thought to have contrived, the duke of Northumberland had entire control over the king, whom, in his last sickness, he persuaded to settle the succession of the crown on the lady Jane Grey (married to the duke's fourth son, lord Guildford Dudley.) On king Edward's death, the duke caused the lady Jane to be proclaimed queen; but his haughty hopes being frustrated by the superior strength of the princess Mary's party, the duke was committed to the Tower, found guilty of high-treason, and executed on the 22nd August 1553. By the attainder, Knole and its appurtenances came again into the hands of the crown.

Queen Mary granted the manor, house and lands of Knole (with other manors) to cardinal Pole, then archbishop of Canterbury, during his natural life, and for one year after, as he should by will direct; and the cardinal, who survived his royal mistress but a few hours, on the 17th November 1558, died possessed of these manors and estates, which thus again became vested in the crown.

Queen Elizabeth, by her letters patent, dated March 1st, in the third year of her reign, granted the manor and house of Knole, with other estates, to Sir Robert Dudley, knt., afterwards earl of Leicester, to hold the same *in capite* by knights' service; all which the earl again surrendered to the queen in the eighth year of her reign.

Soon after this surrender, the queen granted the reversion and fee-simple of these estates (subject to the expiry of two leases therein, one granted by the duke of Northumberland, and the other by the earl of Leicester) to Thomas Sackville, esq., afterwards baron Buckhurst and earl of Dorset.

By virtue of one of the leases above referred to, two at least of the family of

Lennard (of Chevening) occupied Knole
House for some time: Sampson Lennard, esq.
resided here till after the year 1603; and
on the expiry of his term, surrendered the
estate to the queen's grantee, Thomas Sackville, then baron Buckhurst, and lord high
treasurer, of whose history we have spoken
at large in a subsequent page.

The manor and estate of Knole became
thus first possessed by one of the family of
Sackville. It is stated in several publica-
tions as a current tradition, said to have
been "delivered down from the first earl,"
that the queen's motive in bestowing this
house on lord Buckhurst was, " to keep
him near her court and councils, that he
might repair thither on any emergency,
with more expedition than he could from
his seat of Buckhurst in Sussex, the roads
in which county were at times impassable ;"
and it is argued that this account is probable, because no other reason can be
assigned for his quitting Buckhurst (to
which Knole was barely equal, either in
size or grandeur, while it was inferior in

climate,) except the advantage it gave him of being more actively serviceable to his country.

It must be recollected, however, that the queen's grant was to Thomas Sackville, *esquire*, in the eighth or ninth year of her reign (anno 1568 or 1569), who does not appear to have been at that time of her majesty's council. It must also be observed, that supposing the queen's motive to have been as stated, her wishes were most grievously frustrated; for lord Buckhurst did not get possession of Knole until the year 1603, and certainly never *resided* there until that year, or the year following;* being a period of thirty-six or thirty-seven years from the date of the grant of the estate to him, and the queen being then dead.†

The motive of the grant, however, is now

* By the Sevenoaks' Register, it appears that the Lennard family resided at Knole in 1603; while by the earl of Dorset's will, dated 1607, it is certain that his lordship was then in possession.

† Queen Elizabeth died in March, 1603.

of but little importance: lord Buckhurst first removed from Buckhurst to Knole between the years 1603 and 1605, and from that time used it as his principal residence till his death, which happened in 1608. The water-spouts, which have the initials of his name upon them, are dated, none of them earlier than 1605, and some in 1607.

Lord Buckhurst was created earl of Dorset by king James I, on the 13th of March, in the first year of his reign, anno 1603; and as he died in April 1608, and appears, from various marks about the house, to have been earl of Dorset when those marks were first set up, he could not have resided at Knole for more than five years, and that after the death of queen Elizabeth.

The earl was succeeded by his son Robert, who however died in the following year; when the earldom and estates descended to Richard, his son and heir, by Margaret, daughter of Thomas, duke of Norfolk. This nobleman, the third earl of Dorset, became so excessive in his bounties, and so prodigal in his housekeeping, that he was necessitated to sell his estates, and Knole was conveyed by him, about the year 1612, to Henry Smith, esq., citizen and alderman of London, the earl, however, reserving to himself and his heirs, a lease at an annual rent.

This Mr. Smith, who was born and buried at Wandsworth, in Surrey, was a gentleman famed for his extensive charities, given both during his lifetime, and by his last will, and benefiting almost *every* parish in his native county (Surrey), and many in other counties. To effect his benevolent object, he limited his own expenditure during life within a certain stipend; the surplus of his estates being vested in trustees for charitable purposes, as he by his last will, or in default thereof, as they should determine. There is a monument to his memory on the east wall of Wandsworth church, beneath which is his effigy in the attitude of prayer, and an inscription detailing his numerous benefactions; from which it appears that, during his life, he gave to the towns of Croydon, Kingston, Guildford, Dorking, and Farnham, £1000 each, to buy lands in perpetuity for the relief and setting poor people to work in the said towns; and by his will, £1000 to the town of Reigate, and £500 to the town of Wandsworth, for the like purposes; £1000 to buy lands in perpetuity, " to redeem poor captives and prisoners from the Turkish tyranny," with numerous other legacies, for the relief of poor prisoners, soldiers and sailors, the marriage of poor maidens, apprenticeships, repairing highways, aiding the poor and aged, orphans, and persons with large families, &c.

To assist in effecting these most christian intentions, the manor and estate of Knole were assigned, with other estates, to certain noblemen and gentlemen appointed by Mr. Smith as his trustees. By the last will of that gentleman, dated 24th April, 1627, he gave some directions as to part of his estates; but left the bulk of them, among which were the manor, mansion, park and lands of Knole, to the disposal of his trustees; who, in 1641, by deed enrolled in chancery, allotted the rent of Knole manor, house and park, then let to the earl of Dorset at £100 per annum, to be annually distributed among five parishes in Surrey.

Richard, third earl of Dorset, died in 1624, without male issue, and was succeeded by his brother Edward, who appears to have resided at Knole the greater part of his life.

Edward, earl of Dorset, was succeeded, in 1652, by his son and heir, Richard, the fifth earl, who married Lady Frances Cranfield, eldest daughter of Lionel, earl of Middlesex, and eventually sole heir of her brother Lionel, third earl of Middlesex. There seems no doubt that the fifth earl also resided much at Knole, which is confirmed by the arms of Cranfield being over the gateway, on a sun-dial in the garden, and in other places, with those of Sackville; by the circumstance that the furniture presented by king James I, to the earl of Middlesex, when lord-treasurer, (and which descended to his daughter, the fifth

D

countess of Dorset,) still ornaments one of the state rooms of the mansion; and still more convincingly, by the fact, that the manor and estate of Knole, alienated by Richard, the third earl, were redeemed by Richard (his nephew), of whom we are now speaking. This was effected in the thirteenth year of king Charles II, anno 1763, under an act of parliament obtained for that purpose, by virtue of which the trustees of Henry Smith, esq., re-assigned the fee-simple of the manor of Knole, with the mansion, park and lands, to Richard, earl of Dorset, for an adequate consideration applicable to the purposes of the charity—namely, a perpetual clear yearly rent-charge of £130.

Since that period, the manor and estate of Knole have continued in the uninterrupted possession of the Sackville family, of the chief members of which we are now to speak.

Fire-dog in the Cartoon Gallery.

## THE FAMILY OF SACKVILLE.

THE Sackvilles have been persons of wealth and power in this country from the date of the Norman conquest; and in Normandy were lords of the town and seignory

of Sackville, anciently Salchivilla, Salca-
villa, and Saccavilla. Herbrand de Sacke-
ville, (as the name was originally written,)
was one of the chieftains in the army of the
Conqueror. He had three sons, of whom
Sir William, his second son, resided and
possessed considerable estates in England.
His brother, Sir Robert, succeeded him ;
from whom descended Andrew Sackville, esq,
who, in the twenty-fifth year of Edward I,
was summoned to attend the king, with
horse and arms, beyond the seas, and again
in the twenty-ninth year of the same reign,
against the Scotch. For his services on
these occasions, he was knighted in Westminster, by the king's eldest son, the earl
of Carnarvon.

Sir Andrew Sackville was succeeded by
his son, named after him. He served in the
French wars under Edward the Black
Prince, and was knighted in the eighth
year of Edward III. He was sheriff for
the counties of Sussex and Surrey, and
returned to parliament as member for the
former county.

Thomas Sackville, his son by a second wife, was his heir. He also was knighted, anno 1st Richard II, returned member for Bucks the same year, and was sheriff of Sussex and Surrey in the seventh year of Henry IV. Sir Thomas afterwards participated in the dangers and victories of king Henry V. He died in 1432, and was succeeded by his son, Edward, who died in 1459, leaving Humphrey his son and heir, whose son, Richard, was sheriff of Sussex and Surrey, and in the tenth year of Henry VIII, was treasurer of the army in France. He died in 1524, and was buried at Wythiam. His lady was Isabel, daughter of John Digges, esq., of Barham, in Kent, by whom he left issue four sons and six daughters. The youngest, Isabel, was the last prioress of St. Mary's, Clerkenwell.

John Sackville, esq., the next heir, was thrice sheriff of Sussex and Surrey, in the 19th, 32nd, and 39th Henry VIII, and sat in parliament, in the 4th and 5th Philip and Mary, for East Grinstead. He married Anne, second daughter of Sir William

Boleyn, and sister of queen Anne Boleyn, by whom he had issue several sons and daughters. Of the sons, two only lived to maturity. He died in 1537, and was succeeded by his son Richard.

Richard Sackville was a man distinguished in his day both for his talents and his wealth. He was treasurer of the army in the reign of Henry VIII, and chancellor of the Court of Augmentations. He was knighted in the second year of Edward VI, and was of the privy-council to that young monarch, as well as to queens Mary and Elizabeth. Sir Richard served in the parliament which met at Oxford, in the first year of queen Mary; for the county of Kent, in the first of Elizabeth; and in the next parliament for Sussex, which county he afterwards represented during his life. He was likewise under-treasurer of the Exchequer. He died in the eighth year of queen Elizabeth, anno 1566,* and was buried

---

* Erroneously stated to be 1556, in Collins's and Burke's Peerage, Hasted's Kent, and several other authorities.

at Wythiam, in Sussex. His lady was
Winifred, daughter of Sir John Bruges, knt.,
lord-mayor of London in 1520, by whom
he left a son and heir, Thomas, and a
daughter.

His son, Thomas Sackville, esq., afterwards baron Buckhurst and earl of Dorset,
was a student at both the universities, where
he became celebrated for poetic talent. He
was first of Oxford, but afterwards removed
to Cambridge. Thence he went to the Inner
Temple; it being then fashionable for every
young man of fortune, before he began his
travels, or was admitted into parliament, to
be initiated in the study of the law. He
carried with him to the Inner Temple his
love of poetry, and while pursuing his legal
studies, or perhaps *instead* of pursuing them,
.he composed a tragedy called " Ferrex and
Porrex," which was exhibited in the great
hall of the Inner Temple, by the students
of that society, as part of the entertainment
of a grand Christmas festival, and afterwards before queen Elizabeth, at Whitehall. It is remarkable that this was the

first dramatic piece of any note in English
verse; and in estimating its merits, it must
be remembered that it was written many
years before any of Shakspeare's plays. Its
original title was " The Tragedie of Ferrex
and Porrex, sons of Gorboduc;" and it is supposed that the author was assisted in it by
Norton, a fellow-labourer of Sternhold and
Hopkins, to whom parts of the first three
acts are attributed. This tragedy was sur-
reptitiously and incorrectly printed in 1565;
more correctly in 1570; and again in 1590,
when it was entitled " Gorboduc." It was
republished by Dodsley in 1736, with a
preface by Mr. Spence, at the suggestion
of Pope, who " wondered that the propriety
and natural ease of it had not been better
imitated by the dramatic authors of the
succeeding age." It is added, that Mr. Pope
had so high an opinion of this drama that,
at his recommendation, it was brought forward at Drury-lane theatre, and acted with
great success; and Sir Philip Sidney, in
his " Apology for Poetry" gives this lofty
character of it :—" it is full of high-sounding

phrases, climbing to the heights of Seneca's style, and as full of notable morality, which it most delightfully doth teach, and so obtain the very end of poesy." Its popularity was probably increased by the courtly politics it taught; but it is no light praise to the author, that he was the first to reject scriptural subjects, or mysteries, and to strike into history for dramatic amusement.

Mr. Sackville was also, in his early years, the originator of a poem (to which he wrote an introduction), under the title of " The Mirrour of Magistrates." It was intended to comprehend a view of all the illustrious but unfortunate characters of English history, from the date of the Conquest. He found leisure to complete only what he called the " Induction" and one legend, being the life of Henry Stafford, duke of Buckingham. He sketched the plan of the work, and commenced it: it was afterwards left to other hands. Of what he *did* perform, Mr. Warton says, it approached, in richness of allegoric description, nearer to

the style of Spenser than any previous
poem.

In the fourth and fifth year of the reign of
queen Mary, and the first and fifth of Elizabeth, Mr. Sackville served in parliament
for Westmoreland, Sussex, and Bucking-
hamshire. This was during his father's life-
time; of whose death he was apprised at
Rome, where he is said to have been found
in prison, but for what cause is not known.
His liberation was, however, soon obtained,
and he returned to England to take possession of his large inheritance. In the following year, queen Elizabeth granted him the
reversion of the manor-house and park of
Knole as already mentioned. On the 8th
of June in the same year (1567), he was
knighted in the presence of the queen by
the duke of Norfolk, and on the same day
was advanced to the title of lord Buckhurst, baron of Buckhurst,* in the county
of Sussex, and afterwards made knight of

---

* Where his lordship was born.

the Garter. The queen ever afterwards distinguished him with particular marks of her favour. He is said to have been a most perfect and accomplished gentleman, as well in person as in endowments. He was in his youth much disposed to extravagance; and being in the fourteenth year of queen Elizabeth's reign sent ambassador-extraordinary to Charles IX of France, to negociate the marriage contemplated, or pretended to be contemplated, between the queen and the duke of Anjou, his prodigality on the occasion is stated to have been almost ruinous. The indignity of being detained without ceremony in the outer office of a money-lending citizen is said to have been the first hint to reclaim him from his expensive habits; and it is believed that the kind remonstrances of the queen herself, to whom he was related by affinity, were not wanting, to divert him from his immoderate courses. But, whatever were the incentives, his amendment was complete, and advancing years brought increase of estate as well as of honours.

In 1572, lord Buckhurst was one of the peers who sat on the trial of Thomas, duke of Norfolk, who was attainted of high treason, for his communications with Mary, queen of Scots, and beheaded. In 1586, he was one of the commissioners for the trial of the queen of Scots; soon after which he was sent ambassador-extraordinary to the States of the United Provinces, to settle the differences between those States and the earl of Leicester. His conduct on this mission appears to have excited the animosity of the earl of Leicester, at whose instigation lord Buckhurst was recalled to England, and ordered by the queen to remain a close prisoner within his own house. This endured for some months, and but for the earl of Leicester's death, would probably not have terminated so soon. It is alleged on the authority of his chaplain, that during this confinement, lord Buckhurst would not allow his wife, or any of his family to see him. After the earl's death, however, he was speedily restored to the queen's favour, at whose special recommendation he was

elected, in 1591, the successor of Sir
Christopher Hatton, in the chancellorship
of Oxford. While residing at Oxford, the
queen honoured him with a visit of several
days, during which she was entertained
with great magnificence, with speeches,
plays, &c.

In 1598, he was joined with lord Burleigh to negociate a peace with Spain; on
which occasion his abilities were so eminently displayed as to lead to his elevation
to the office of lord-high-treasurer, to which
he was appointed on the death of Burleigh.
From this period he acted with Sir Robert
Cecil to the end of Elizabeth's reign, and
is said to have been eminently serviceable
to her majesty in detecting and defeating
the ambitious projects of the earl of Essex.
In the forty-third of Elizabeth, he presided as lord-high-steward at the trial of
the earls of Essex and Southampton, and
in passing sentence upon Essex, advised
him in the most impressive manner to
appeal to the queen's mercy. The next
year he was appointed one of the lords

commissioners for exercising the office of earl-marshal of England.

On the accession of king James, he was confirmed in the office of treasurer, continued to co-operate with Cecil, and in the first year of that reign was created earl of Dorset. He continued · his attention to affairs of state to the last hour of his life, and died at the council-table, April 19th, 1608, aged about 75. He was buried at Wythiam, in Sussex. His death made way for James's Scotch favourites, and laid the foundation of the ruin of that king's race.

All biographers are agreed in awarding to this great man an unimpeachable character in all the relations of private life: he was a benefactor to the poor, a liberal landlord, "an affectionate husband, a kind father, and a firm friend."* As a statesman, he was distinguished for political independence, notwithstanding that he stood so high in the queen's good graces, that he might be presumed to be devoted entirely

* Walpole.

to her service. It would seem to have been on account of his strict integrity that her majesty continued to place the greatest confidence in him, and to employ him in the most important affairs up to the day of her death. As a speaker and writer, of the age in which he lived, he is entitled to the highest respect. He is said to have himself composed nearly all his state-papers, and he unquestionably made valuable improvements in the style and taste of English poetry. Several of his letters are preserved in the *Cabala*, and one to the earl of Sussex, is printed in the Howard collection, p. 297.

His lordship married Cecile, daughter of Sir John Baker, knt., of Sissinghurst, with whom he lived in uninterrupted harmony for fifty-one years, and left issue by her four sons and three daughters.

His eldest son, Robert, succeeded as earl of Dorset, and likewise to the inheritance of Knole; but he died the following year, aged 48, and was buried with his ancestors at Wythiam, in Sussex. He was a man of science and a linguist, and had considerable

influence in the Commons' house of parliament, where he served for the borough of
East Grinstead, and subsequently for the
county of Sussex. By his last will, he left
£1000, or as much as might be necessary,
for founding an hospital at East Grinstead
(called Sackville College), for thirty-one
poor persons, and endowed it with £390 a
year. He was twice married; but had issue
by his first lady only (Margaret, daughter
of Thomas, duke of Norfolk), who bore
him three sons and three daughters. His
second son, Richard, succeeded him, his
elder brother having died in the father's life
time.

Richard, third earl of Dorset, had not
attained his twentieth year when he inherited
the earldom and estates. Within two days
after his father's death he married the celebrated lady Anne Clifford, daughter and
heiress of George Clifford, earl of Cumberland, the lady being in her nineteenth year.
The reason for this indecent haste does not
appear; but it seems that, two years afterwards, agreeably to some engagement made

with his friends before his marriage, he went abroad, though with what object is also a secret;—if in the hope of gaining wisdom or prudence, his friends were not gratified; for he returned to Knole on the 8th of April, 1612, from which period, with all the impetuosity of youth possessed of means apparently inexhaustible, he led a life of most profuse magnificence and unbounded hospitality. The consequences may be readily anticipated,—he was compelled to sell his possessions; among the rest were the manor of Sevenoaks, previously purchased by him of Henry Carey, lord Hunsdon, and the manor, seat, and park of Knole, of which, however, he reserved to himself and his heirs a lease. He is described as handsome in person, elegant in manners, and generous in disposition, possessed of considerable learning, though of but little prudence, affable, and kind. His lady, who survived him, and was afterwards married to Philip Herbert, earl of Pembroke (whom she also survived), thus speaks of him:—" This first lord of mine was in

his own nature of a just mind, of a sweet
disposition, and very valiant in his own
person. He had a great advantage in his
breeding by the wisdom and devotion of
his grandfather, Thomas Sackville, earl of
Dorset, and lord-high-treasurer, who was
one of the wisest men of that time, by which
means he was so good a scholar in all manner of learning, that in his youth, when he
was in the university of Oxford, there were
none of the young nobility that excelled
him. He was also a good patriot to his
country, and generally beloved in it; much
esteemed of in all the parliaments that sat
in his time; and so great a lover of scholars
and soldiers, as that with an excessive bounty
towards them, or indeed any of worth that
were in distress, he did much diminish his
estate, as also with excessive prodigality in
house-keeping and other noble ways at
court, as tilting, masking, and the like,
prince Henry being then alive, who was
much addicted, to those noble exercises,
and of whom he was much beloved."

Of the state in which this young noble-

man lived, some conception may be formed
from a catalogue of his household and
family, from 1613 to 1624, copied by
Mr. Bridgman, from a manuscript in Knole
House. From this it appears, that at "my
lord's" table, there sat daily eight persons;
at the parlour table, twenty-one, including
ladies in waiting, chaplain, secretary, pages,
&c.; at the clerk's table in the hall, twenty,
consisting of the principal household officers; in the nursery, four; at the long
table in the hall, forty-eight, being attendants, footmen, and other inferior domestics;
at the laundry-maid's table, twelve, and in
the kitchen and scullery, six:—in all, a
constant household of one-hundred and nineteen persons, independently of visiters.
Dorset House, London, situate where Salis-
bury-square now stands, was also maintained at the same time, besides a seat called
Bolebroke House in Sussex. His lordship
died at his town-house on the 18th March
1624, at the early age of thirty-five, and
was buried at Wythiam, in Sussex. He
had issue three sons and two daughters:

but the sons having died in infancy, he was succeeded in the earldom and wreck of the estates by Sir Edward Sackville, K.B., his only surviving brother.

Edward, fourth earl of Dorset, was born in 1590. He was educated with his brother Richard, and in his youth distinguished for his abilities. Soon after he came of age, he married Mary, daughter and heiress of Sir George Curzon, of Croxhall, in Derbyshire. Two years after this, namely in 1613, being then at Croxhall, he was concerned in a fatal duel, which is thus mentioned by lord Clarendon:—" He entered into a fatal quarrel, upon a subject very unwarrantable, with a young nobleman of Scotland, the lord Bruce, upon which they both transported themselves into Flanders, and, attended only by two chirurgiens, placed at a distance, and under an obligation not to stir but at the fall of one of them, they fought under the walls of Antwerp, when the lord Bruce fell dead upon the place; and Mr. Sackville being likewise hurt, retired into the next monastery which was at hand."

This affair having naturally excited great attention at the time, and many injurious reports being in circulation, Mr. Sackville, before his return to England, explained in a letter, "on the faith of a gentleman," all the details of the duel, and sent it to a friend to be delivered to the lord-chamberlain. From this statement, which carries with it the strongest marks of punctilious veracity, it appears that the parties met at Bergen-op-Zoom, lord Bruce accompanied by Mr. Crawford, an English gentleman, for his second, a surgeon and his man, and Mr. Sackville accompanied by Sir John Heydon, knt. Lord Bruce then addressing himself to Sir John Heydon, told him, "that he found himself so behind-hand, that a little of his (Mr. Sackville's) blood would not serve his turn, and that he therefore was now resolved to have him *alone*, to satisfy himself, and his honours." It was finally agreed, in spite of the indignant remonstrances of Sir John Heydon on such blood-thirsty intentions, that the principals should ride on together for two miles,

attended by their surgeons only, they being
unarmed.    Mr. Sackville then relates the
manner of the death-fight in the following
words :—

"I being then very mad with anger the
lord Bruce should thirst after my life with
a kind of assuredness, bade him alight,
which with all willingness he quickly
granted; and there, in a meadow (ancle-
deep in the water at least), bidding farewell
to our doublets, in our shirts we began to
charge each other, having afore commanded
our surgeons to withdraw themselves a
pretty distance from us; conjuring them
besides, as they respected our favour or
their own safeties, not to stir, but suffer us
to execute our pleasure; we being fully
resolved (God forgive us) to despatch each
other by what means we could.  I made a
thrust at my enemy, but was short; and in
drawing back my arm, I received a great
wound thereon; but, in revenge, I pressed
into him, though I then missed him also;
and then received a wound in my right pap,
which passed level through my body, and

almost to my back ; and there we wrestled
for the two greatest and dearest prizes,
honour and life; in which struggling, my
hand, having but an ordinary glove on it,
lost one of her servants, though the meanest,
which hung by a skin. But at last breath-
ing, yet keeping our holds, there passed on
both sides propositions of quitting each
other's sword. But, when amity was dead,
confidence could not live, and who should
quit first was the question; and, re-striving
again afresh, with a kick and a wrench
together, I freed my long-captive weapon,
which incontinently levying at his throat,
being master still of his, I demanded if he
would ask his life or yield his sword? Both
which, though in that imminent danger,
he bravely denied to do. Myself being
wounded, and feeling loss of blood, having
three conduits running on me, began to make
me faint; and he courageously persisting
not to accord to either of my propositions,
from remembrance of his former bloody
desire, and feeling of my present estate, I
struck at his heart: but, with his avoiding,

missed my aim, yet passed through his body, and, drawing back my sword repassed it again through another place, when he cried, 'Oh, I am slain!' seconding his speech with all the force he had to cast me. But being too weak, after I had defended his assault, I easily became master of him, laying him on his back; when being upon him, I re-demanded, if he would request his life? But it seems he prized it not at so dear a rate to be beholden for it, bravely replying 'He scorned it!' which answer of his was so noble and worthy, as I protest I could not find in my heart to offer him any more violence, only keeping him down, till, at length, his surgeon afar off cried out, 'He would immediately die if his wounds were not stopped!' Whereupon I asked, 'if he desired his surgeon should come?' which he accepted of; and so being drawn away, I never offered to take his sword, accounting it inhumane to rob a dead man, for so I held him to be. This thus ended, I retired to my surgeon, in whose arms, after I had remained awhile for want of blood, I lost my sight, and withal, as I then thought, my life also. But strong water and his diligence quickly recovered me; when I escaped a great danger, for my lord's surgeon, when nobody dreamt of it, came full at me with his lord's sword, and had not mine with my sword interposed himself, I had been slain by those base hands, although my lord Bruce, weltering in his blood, and past all expectation of life, conformable to all his former carriage, which was undoubtedly noble, cried out, 'Rascal, hold thy hand!' So may I prosper as I have dealt sincerely with you in this relation.

"EDWARD SACKVILLE.

"*Lovain, the 8th September,* 1613."

The cause of this butcherly conflict has never transpired: lord Clarendon, who is supposed to have known it, contents himself by saying that it was "upon a subject very unwarrantable."

In November, 1616, Mr. Sackville was created a knight of the Bath, and about the

G

same period, elected member for the county of Sussex. In 1620, he was one of the principal commanders of the forces then sent to the assistance of Frederick, king of Bohemia, and was in the celebrated battle of Prague, fought that year. On the 12th March, 1621, Sir Edward Sackville advocated, in the House of Commons, the cause of lord Bacon, then charged with corruption. In the same year he went out as ambassador to Louis XIIIth of France; after which he was elevated by king James to a seat at the privy council. He was abroad when he succeeded to the earldom of Dorset, the estates of which he found so encumbered, that but little was left for the support of the dignity.

His lordship, however, immediately returned to England; and, after the accession of king Charles I, he was, on the 15th May, 1625, installed a knight of the Garter, and on that king's marriage, made lord-chamberlain to the queen (as he was afterwards to the king), being then a privy-councillor, and joint lord-lieutenant of Sussex. In

1640, he was one of the regents during the king's absence in Scotland, and at the same time lord-lieutenant of Middlesex; in which latter capacity he incurred the displeasure of the House of Commons, by ordering the train-bands to fire upon a mob which was collected to intimidate the House of Lords, when the bill against the bishops was under discussion. In 1641, he was president of the council and lord-privy-seal, and during the whole of the contest which ensued, between king Charles and his parliament, he remained loyal and stedfast to that unfortunate monarch; attended him at the battle of Edge-hill, addressed the council in his favour in 1643, was with him when he surrendered himself to the Scottish army, and finally, was one of his most faithful adherents when he was, in 1647, taken to Hampton Court. After this, the king being virtually in the hands of the army, and his fatal end rapidly approaching, the earl of Dorset, and his other noble attendants, were forcibly separated from the royal person. After the death of his sovereign, the earl never quitted his house, but dying on the 17th July, 1652, was buried with his ancestors at Wythiam. Of his character we have the following summary by lord Clarendon: "his wit sparkling and sublime; his other parts of such lustre, that he could not miscarry in the world. He had a very sharp discerning spirit, and was a man of an obliging nature, much honour, of great generosity, and of most entire fidelity to the crown."

His lordship suffered grievously by his honest devotion to the royal cause: in 1625, his son, Edward, being taken prisoner by the parliamentary forces, was barbarously murdered; and in the same year he was deprived of his estate of Knole, the parliamentary commissioners having held a court in the dining-parlour, in order to its sequestration. It had previously been plundered by the troops; and indeed it is wonderful, under the circumstances, that the place escaped so well as it did.

His lordship had issue a daughter, Mary, who died young; and two sons, Edward, of whose untimely fate we have just spoken, and Richard, his successor.

Richard, fifth earl of Dorset, was born in 1622. During his father's lifetime, he was one of the fifty-nine members of the House of Commons who voted against the attainder of the earl of Strafford. He married lady Frances, daughter of Lionel earl of Cranfield and Middlesex, and eventually inheriting the estates of her brother, Lionel, earl of Middlesex. The date of this marriage does not appear; neither can we find any record of the earl's actions during the troublous times of the commonwealth, except that Mr. Bridgman quotes the following documents, the originals of which are at Knole, in proof that his circumstances were not much to be envied.

" To his highness y^e lord protector of the commonwealth of England, Scotland, and Ireland, the several answers of Richard, earle of Dorsett, to the petition of the poor creditors of Edward, late earle of of Dorsett, deceased,

"Humbly sheweth,

"That this respondent was and is a mere stranger to the actions and engagements of the said Edward, earle of Dorsett, his late father, charged upon this respondent in the said petition, from whom this respondent hath not, nor ever had, aine assetts, either reall or personall; but this respondent's said father, at the tyme of his death, was, by an engagement under his hand and seale, really and *bona fide* indebted to this respondent in the sum of £1200 and upwards, w^ch this respondent hath utterly lost, without any hopes of ever being satisfied for the same. And as to the pretended combination with Major Basse, or anie unjust practicings, or confederacy, by and of this resp^t with any other person or persons whatever, or this respon^t's voluptuous living, alledged in the said petition, this respon^t absolutely denyeth the same to be true, and humbly averreth that the said allegations and inferences are merely false and scandalous; and therefore this respon^t humbly prayes y^r highness that he may be dismissed.

"And this respon^t shall ever pray."

" Pulletry,

" Wher'as, by o$^r$ warrant, wee lately˙ commanded you that you should arrest the body of Richard, earl of Dorsett, soe that wee might have his body before the barons of the Exchequer at Westminster, in eight dayes of St. Hilary next coming, to answer unto the lord-protector of divers trespasses, contempts, and offencies, by him lately done and committed : Now, for that the said Richard, earl of Dorsett, hath put in baile unto us to appear before the barons afore-said, at the day and place aforesaid, there-fore wee command you that you forbear execucion of the said warrant, or any wayes to arrest, molest, or trouble the said earl, o$^r$ said warrant unto you formerly in any wise notwithstanding.

"Dated 12-3, 1656.

" To any of o$^r$ serjeants at mace,

"NATHANIEL TIMMS,⎱
"TEMPEST MILNER, ⎰ Sheriffs."

After the death of Cromwell, which happened in 1658, we find the earl of Dorset following up the loyal principles of his father, and a chief promoter of the restoration of king Charles II, which being effected, he was, in 1660, joined with the earl of Berkshire in the lord-lieutenancy of Middlesex and Westminster; and in October of the same year he was commissioned with other lords to try the regicides.

In 1661, he was admitted, with the duke of York, of the Inner Temple; and in the course of the same year (having previously, as is presumed, become possessed of considerable property in right of his wife), he re-purchased the manor, mansion and park, of Knole, which he made his chief residence. He does not appear to have held any office at the court of Charles II; but in 1670, he was constituted, jointly with lord Buckhurst, his son, lord-lieutenant and custos rotulorum of the county of Sussex. He died August 27, 1677, and was succeeded by his eldest son, Charles.

Charles, sixth earl of Dorset, had, two years anterior to his father's death, become possessed, in right of his mother, of the estates of his uncle, the earl of Middlesex, who died in 1674, in consequence of which he had been, by letters patent, dated 4th April, 1675, created baron Cranfield, of Cranfield in the county of Bedford, and earl of Middlesex. His lordship is stated by Mr. Bridgman to have been born on the 24th January, 1637; but no authority is to be found for this date, which is evidently erroneous, as his father, according to Bridgman himself, and many other authorities, was not born until September, 1622. It seems probable, however, that he was nearly forty years of age in 1677, when he succeeded his father as earl of Dorset; for, shortly after the restoration of Charles II, which took place in 1660, he served as member for East Grinstead, and may be presumed to have been then of full age. Subsequently to this, he became a great favourite with king Charles II, to whom he recommended himself by his generous disposition, elegant manners, the sprightliness of his wit, and we fear we must add, his accomplished libertinism. He was privately educated, and after making the grand tour, returned to England a little before the Restoration. He soon distinguished himself as a speaker in the House of Commons, and was, besides, greatly admired for his Anacreontic poetry. The king offered him employment under the government, but he was too much bent on the gratification of his pleasures to engage in anything like business. Associating with Villiers, Rochester, Sedley, Ogle, and other fashionable libertines, he entered into much of their profligacy, and is mentioned as one of the party in many anecdotes which reflect disgrace on the young nobility of that day.

In 1665, on the breaking out of the Dutch war, Sackville first awoke to manly exertion. He placed himself as a volunteer under the duke of York, and behaved with great gallantry in the action of the 3rd of June, when the Dutch admiral, Opdam, was blown up, and many ships taken or destroyed. It was on the evening preceding this engagement, that he composed the well-known song

"To all you ladies now on land."

Soon after this he was made a gentleman of the bed-chamber, and sent repeatedly to France on embassies of compliment.

After the death of king Charles II, the earl of Dorset retired from court; but he was present with other noblemen at the King's Bench, on the 29th June, 1688, at the trial of the bishops, and was warmly engaged in the measures which brought on the Revolution, and placed William and Mary on the throne. He accompanied the princess Anne of Denmark on her flight from her father's court, attended her to Northampton, and there provided her with a body-guard of horsemen. On the acknowledgment of the prince and princess of Orange, as king and queen of these realms, the earl of Dorset was sworn of the privy-council, and made lord-chamberlain of the household. He was elected a knight of the Garter, and accompanied the king to Holland in 1691; and he had the honour of

being four times appointed one of the
regents of the kingdom during his majesty's
absence. About 1698, he withdrew from
public life, and spent the remainder of his
days in retirement. He died at Bath on
the 29th January, 1706, and was buried in
the family vault at Wythiam.

Horace Walpole, in speaking of this
nobleman, says "he was the first gentleman in the voluptuous court of Charles II,
and in the gloomy one of king William.
He had as much wit at his first master,
or his cotemporaries Buckingham and Rochester, without the king's want of feeling,
the duke's want of principle, or the earl's
want of thought." All are agreed in
awarding to him talents and accomplishments of the first order, with a disposition
generous to excess. He was a constant and
munificent patron of men of learning and
genius—the Mæcenas of his time. Prior,
Dryden, Butler, Congreve, Wycherly, Addison and Pope, all write in his praise; many
of them in a style, which, to say the least
of it, is sufficiently flattering. Of these

writers, the first two had partaken largely
of his bounty, as they frankly acknowledge;
Prior gratefully avowing "that he scarcely
knew what life was, until he found himself
obliged by his lordship's favour." Killigrew, also, was much indebted to him; and
Durfey, who for some years had apartments
at Knole, had repeated proofs of his kind-
ness. To his lordship's character for generosity, must therefore certainly be assigned
much of the too-fulsome panegyric with
which men of genius, who dined at his
table, have addressed him. Dryden, one
of his chief admirers, in the attempt to pro-
duce authors of our own country superior to
those of antiquity, vents the following gross
adulation, " I would instance your lordship
in satire, and Shakspeare in tragedy !"

The epitaph written by Pope, com-
mencing—

" Dorset, the grace of courts, the muses' pride"—

is too well known for quotation: and, like
the tributes of other less independent pane-
gyrists, is certainly most complimentary.

If the following pleasant anecdote be
true, it would seem that his lordship was
himself fully aware that the surest mode of
bearing away the palm was to gratify the
umpire. It was agreed by a party assembled at Knole, that each should write an
impromptu, and that Dryden should decide
which was the best. All present, except
the earl, went studiously to work; meantime his lordship wrote a few hasty words,
and threw the paper upon the table. The
contribution of each having been obtained,
Dryden rose and said, that he was sure the
company would unanimously agree with
him that nothing could surpass the earl's,
which he begged to read to them:—" I
promise to pay Mr. John Dryden, or order,
five hundred pounds, on demand. Dorset."

The earl was twice married; first, to
Elizabeth, daughter of Hervey Bagot, esq.,
of Pipe Hall, Cumberland, (and widow of
Charles Berkeley, earl of Falmouth,) by
whom he had no issue; secondly, to lady
Mary, daughter of James Compton, earl of
Northampton, who bore him a son, Lionel

Cranfield, his successor, and a daughter, Mary, who married Henry Somerset, duke of Beaufort.

Lionel Cranfield, the seventh earl and first duke of Dorset, was born on the 18th of January, 1688. In 1706, being then in his nineteenth year, he went to Hanover with the earl of Halifax, who was the bearer of the act of settlement from queen Anne to the Electorate. In 1708, he was appointed constable of Dover Castle, and lord-warden of the Cinque-Ports. At the demise of queen Anne, he was sent ambassador to Hanover to announce that event to the Elector (who thereby succeeded to the English throne as George I), and to attend his majesty on his journey to England. He was forthwith sworn of the privy-council, constituted first gentleman of the bed-chamber, and a few days afterwards, October 16, 1714, was installed a knight of the Garter. In 1720, he was advanced to the dignity of duke of Dorset. In 1724, he was made custos rotulorum of the county of Kent, and next year lord-steward of the

king's household, and one of the lords
justices during the king's absence from
England; which trust he was several times
honoured with in the succeeding reign of
George II, whenever the king went abroad.
At the coronation of George II, he was
appointed lord-high-steward of England
for the day.

In 1730, he was appointed lord-lieutenant
of Ireland; in 1737, lord-steward of the
household a second time; 1744, lord-president of the council; and in 1746, he was
lord-lieutenant and custos rotulorum of the
county of Kent, and vice-admiral of the
same.

In 1751, the duke was again lord lieu-
tenant of Ireland; resigning which in 1755,
he was appointed master of the horse.
This he gave up in 1757, when the office of
constable of Dover Castle, and lord-warden
of the Cinque Ports was conferred on him
for life. At the accession of king George III,
he was continued of the privy-council, and
in his commission of lord-lieutenant, &c., of
Kent. After which, being greatly advanced

in years, he retired from public employment. He died October 9, 1765, greatly respected, and was buried with his ancestors at Wythiam.

These details are chiefly from Mr. Hasted's History of Kent, to which we must add that, "in private life he united the amiable character of a kind husband and father, with that of an excellent master and a sincere friend. He lived in great hospitality all his life; and when at Knole, the front of the house was frequently crowded with horses and carriages, so as to give it rather the appearance of a princely levee than the residence of a private nobleman."*

His grace married Elizabeth, daughter of lieutenant-general Colyear (brother of David, earl of Portmore), by whom he had six children, three of whom were sons; namely:

I. CHARLES, his successor.

II. John Philip, who married Frances, daughter of John earl Gower, and

---

* Bridgman's Sketch.

dying in 1765, left issue a daughter, and a son, namely

JOHN FREDERICK, who succeeded as third duke.

III. George, afterwards known as lord George Germaine, and still later as viscount Sackville.* He died in 1785, leaving issue,

CHARLES, the *present duke* of Dorset, and four other children.

On the decease of Lionel, first duke of Dorset, his eldest son, Charles, earl of Middlesex, succeeded to his titles and estates. He had previously been M. P. for East Grinstead, and master of the horse to Frederick, prince of Wales. In 1766, he was constituted lord-lieutenant and custos rotulorum of the county of Kent; but he did not long survive. He was a poet, and a connoisseur in the arts: the song of "Arno's vale" attests his merit in the former

* For a biographical notice of this nobleman, see Appendix, No. 49.

capacity. His grace married a daughter of viscount Shannon, but had no issue. He died January 6, 1769, and was succeeded by his nephew John Frederick, the only son of his next brother, John Philip, deceased.

John Frederick, third duke of Dorset, was born in 1745, and consequently was about twenty-four years of age when he inherited the family dignities. His grace had served, like his ancestors, for the borough of East Grinstead; and on his succession to the dukedom, he was appointed lord-lieutenant, &c. of the county, in the place of his late uncle. For many years he mingled but little in political or busy life; his time being devoted to gallantry and pleasure among the fashionable circles, as well in France and Italy, as in England. In 1783, his grace was ambassador to the court of France, where he continued some years, until the dawn of the revolution which convulsed that kingdom. At the time of the king's serious illness in 1789, when Mr. Fox's party claimed as a right the regency for the prince of Wales, we find the duke of Dorset exerting himself in support of Mr. Pitt's measures. He was a knight of the Garter, and lord-steward of the household. His grace remained a bachelor until 1790, when he married Arabella-Diana, daughter and co-heir of sir John Cope, bart., by whom he had three children; namely, George John Frederick, fourth duke; Mary, now countess-dowager of Plymouth, and Elizabeth, present countess Delaware. The third duke died at Knole on the 19th July, 1799. He was much attached to the place, and expended considerable sums in its repair, and internal embellishment, but would not suffer the primitive form and character of its exterior to be altered. Many of the finest plantations in the park were formed under his direction; and a number of valuable pictures and busts purchased by him, and added to the collection in the state-rooms.

The demise of the third duke was succeeded by a long minority, during which, and until her death in 1825, the duchess-dowager of Dorset continued to reside at Knole, by virtue, we believe, of the testamentary dispositions of the duke her husband. Her grace formed a second matrimonial alliance with Charles, earl Whitworth. His lordship was the eldest son of Sir Charles Whitworth, knt., of an ancient Staffordshire family; and having distinguished himself as a diplomatist at the courts of Poland and St. Petersburg, he was, in 1800, created an Irish baron, and subsequently, on his return, in 1814, from Paris (whither he had gone as ambassador-extraordinary), he was made a peer of Great Britain by the title of baron Whitworth, of Adbaston, in the county of Stafford, and in the following year raised to the dignity of an earl.* His lordship succeeded the duke of Richmond as viceroy of Ireland, in 1814; but he resigned in 1817. Earl Whitworth and the duchess-dowager of Dorset both died in the same year, 1825.

---

* Earl Whitworth was also a Knight Grand Cross of the Order of the Bath, civil distinction.

Meantime, her grace's eldest daughter, Mary, had been, in 1811, married to the earl of Plymouth, who died in July, 1833, without issue; her second daughter, Elizabeth, to earl Delawarr, by whom she has now a numerous family; and her son had, in November, 1814, attained his majority, and in February, 1815, had been snatched from the world by a fatal accident.

George John Frederick, fourth duke of Dorset, had not attained his sixth year when his father died. He was for about two years instructed in the rudiments of education by a private tutor, and in his ninth year was entered at Harrow school, where he distinguished himself by uncommon zeal and diligence in his studies, and by his skill and vigour in games and athletic exercises. He was entered of Christ-Church college, Oxford, in 1810; and here he displayed all the good qualities which had given so fair a promise at school, and was persevering in regular habits of alternate study and exercise, when an unfortunate blow received on his right eye from a tennis-ball, obliged him to suspend his literary pursuits, and finally to change the whole course of his studies, and abandon the idea of taking a regular degree. He passed nearly three academical years in the university; and when about to quit, the dean of Christ-Church lamented his departure as " the loss of an example of all that was amiable and proper to the young men of that society."

Soon after leaving Oxford, the young duke accompanied his mother and earl Whitworth to Ireland, of which his lordship had been then appointed lord-lieutenant. The duke had been in Ireland about a year and a half, when he met with the awful accident which put an end to his existence. On the 13th of February, 1815, he went to pay a visit to his friend and school-fellow, lord Powerscourt, intending to stay from the Monday till the Thursday. On the 14th he went out with lord Powerscourt's harriers, mounted on a well-trained Irish mare, and accompanied by his lordship and Mr. Wingfield. Having been out for several hours without finding anything, they were actually on the point of returning home, when a hare sprang up, and the chace commenced. The hare made for the inclosures on Kilkenny Hill. They had gone but a short distance, when the duke, who was an excellent and forward horseman, rode at a wall, which was in fact a more dangerous obstacle than it appeared to be. The wall stands on a slope, and, from the lower ground, what is immediately on the other side cannot be discerned. The wall itself is perhaps no more than three feet and a half in length, and two in breadth; but on the other side there lay a range of large and ponderous stones, which had been rolled there from off the surface of the adjacent barley-field, that they might not impede the growth of the corn. It would have been safer to scramble over such a fence, than to take it in the stroke. The duke's mare, however, attempted to cover all at one spring, and cleared the wall; but, lighting among the stones on the other side, threw herself headlong, and, turning in the air, came with great violence upon her

rider, who had not lost his seat; he under-
most, with his back on one of the large
stones, and she crushing him with all her
weight on his chest, and struggling with all
her might to recover her legs! The mare
at length disentangled herself, and gallopped
away. The duke sprang upon his feet, and
attempted to follow her, but soon found
himself unable to stand, and fell into the
arms of Mr. Farrel, who had run to his
succour, and to whose house he was conveyed. Lord Powerscourt, in the utmost
anxiety and alarm, rode full speed for me-
dical assistance, leaving his brother, Mr.
Wingfield, to pay every possible attention
to the duke. But, unhappily, the injury
was too severe to be counteracted by human
skill: life was extinct before any surgeon
arrived.

Such was the melancholy catastrophe
that caused the untimely death of this
young nobleman. He had been of age
only three months, and had not taken his
seat in the House of Lords. He is described
as having been of gentle and engaging

manners, tinctured with shyness, of amiable temper, warm and steady in his affections, endowed with considerable judgment and penetration, and possessing, with the accomplishments of a perfect gentleman, all the qualities that constitute an honest man.

His grace was succeeded in his titles by Charles Sackville Germaine, viscount Sackville and Baron Bolebroke, son of George, first viscount Sackville, (of whom a memoir is given, Appendix No. 49,) and grandson to Lionel the first duke.

The present duke of Dorset was born on the 27th August, 1767, and succeeded to the viscountcy of Sackville, and barony of Bolebroke, on the death of his father. His grace's full titles are—duke of Dorset, earl of Dorset and Middlesex, viscount Sackville, baron Buckhurst, baron Cranfield, and baron Bolebroke. He is besides a Knight of the Garter. The dates of creation of these several dignities are as follow:

Baron Buckhurst, 8th June, 1567; earl of Dorset, 13th of March, 1603-4; baron Cranfield and earl of Middlesex, 4th April,

1675; duke of Dorset, 13th June, 1720; viscount Sackville and baron Bolebroke, 11th February, 1782.

*Arms.*—Quarterly, or and gules, over all a bend vair.

*Crest.*—Out of a coronet composed of eight fleurs-de-lis, or, an etoile of the like number of points, ar.

*Supporters.*—Two leopards, ar., spotted sa.

*Motto.*—Aut nunquam tentes, aut perfice.

His grace's seat is Drayton House, Northamptonshire. He is unmarried.

It should perhaps be mentioned, that the manor and mansion of Knole form no part of his grace's estate; they having been settled on the late duchess-dowager for her life, and after her decease (the fourth duke of Dorset having died of full age, but unmarried and without issue), devolved on her daughters, the countesses of Plymouth and De Lawarr, as co-heiresses to their lamented brother.

"The Old Oak."

## THE PARK.

THE park of Knole has on the west for
nearly a mile the town of Sevenoaks: it
extends to the north by the Maidstone road
a considerable distance below the town;

and to the south its tall beeches overshadow the Hastings road more than a mile. From the top of Riverhill the road to Seal bounds it on the south and south-east; on the east it has the wild picturesque heath called Fawke, and on the north-east Wildernesse Park and other grounds belonging to the marquess Camden. It encloses an area of nearly one thousand acres, and presents a delightful variety of hill and valley, and high level land.

The additions made by the late earl of Plymouth of the large portion of rich land, formerly called Suffolk Paddock, and the extensive tract thickly matted with brake and furze, near Blackhall, have contributed greatly to increase its beauty; the rough and tangled wildness of the latter affording a pleasing contrast to the smooth verdure of the turf. From the top of this furze-bank, we catch the chimneys and long roofs of the house, prominent above the many broad masses of oak and sycamore and the feathery tops of beech which rise from the intervening valley; and it will

well repay an evening walk to view its
towers and gables standing forth in bold
relief against the setting sun, or the long
lines of the grey twilight clouds.

From the valley beneath, the access to
the mansion is by a long avenue of oaks,
called the Duchess's walk; and the brow
of the opposite hill is crowned for many an
acre with a succession of noble trees: one
of them is an ancient oak, an engraving
of which is placed at the head of this
chapter, which may have sheltered barons
and knights of the era of the elder Plan-
tagenets, in their excursions across the
extensive forests or wastes, of which this
park must have formed a portion, previous
to its enclosure. Two centuries since it
was known as " the old oak," and although
its huge trunk, which measures thirty
feet in circumference, is falling to decay,
yet enough of life remains for us to hope
it may continue " the old oak" for centuries to come. Near it, and among a
group of flowing beeches, whose lofty white
stems rise like stately columns among the

dark shadows of their deep green foliage, stands one beech of immense size, measuring nearly twenty-eight feet in circumference. Near the Ice-house is another remarkable for its beauty, which attracted the notice of Mrs. Radcliffe on a visit to Knole, and, with the adjoining scenery, is thus described by her :—

" In the park, abounding with noble beech groves, is one, on the left of the road leading to the house, which for mass and over-topping pomp, excels even any in Windsor Park, when viewed as you descend from the park gate, whence shade rises above shade, with amazing and magnificent grandeur. In this mass of wood is one beech, that stretches upwards its grey limbs among the light feathery foliage to a height, and with a majesty that is sublime. Over a seat, placed round the bole, it spreads out a light yet umbrageous fan, most graceful and beautiful. With all its grandeur and luxuriance, there is nothing in this beech heavy or formal; it is airy, though vast and majestic, and suggests an idea at once of the strength and fire of a hero! I should call a beech-tree, and this beech above every other—the hero of the forest, as the oak is called the king."

To the south-east of the extensive pleasure-grounds at the back of the mansion, is a small building, in the ecclesiastic style of pointed architecture, surrounded by palisades, and a broken flint wall. Its shape is multangular, having gables and a pointed roof, finished with a lofty spire, and its rooms are very irregularly formed. Above one of the chimney-pieces is some carving, and in the windows are some small figures on glass in relievo, consisting of the apostles and virtues, well drawn, but of late years sorely mutilated. The lower panels of a folding door have some bold heads, and the door of entrance is guarded from witchcraft by an old horseshoe. Scattered about are the apparent remains of the foundations of buildings of a date considerably prior to the dwelling. The stone door and window frames have quite the appearance of antiquity, and were no doubt brought here at the demolition of some ancient building in the neighbourhood. These erections were made under the direction of Captain Smyth, (father of Sir Sydney Smyth,) who resided much at Knole in the time of Charles, second duke of Dorset;[*]

* During the sojourn of Captain Smith at Knole, he was engaged in building Ash Grove, in the vicinity. About this time some alteration was made in the militia law; a meeting of magistrates was held at the Crown Inn, Sevenoaks, to put the new law into operation, and able-bodied men were summoned from every parish within the district, from whom the number required for the public service was to be drawn. The meeting was tumultuous, and every species of insubordination manifested; the magistrates were insulted, and driven from the inn, and the house of the Rev. T. Curteis (grandfather to the present rector) was much damaged by the mob. Mr. C. made his escape through the fields to Knole House, and Captain Smyth, then the only resident, ordered all the gates to be closed, and the mechanics and all employed about the premises to keep within. Meeting with no opposition, and having wreaked their fury upon the rector's property, and driven the magistrates, who were, they supposed, the authors of the obnoxious law, from the place, to make victory complete, they had only to drive away Captain Smyth. The house was assailed by the mob, who, demanding entrance, knocked loudly at the gates, and crying "No militia," re-

and the materials were probably brought from Otford, as a tower, forming a portion of the old palace, was at that period taken down by lord-chief-baron Smythe.

A small collection of foreign birds was

quired that the Doctor should be given up. The captain in the meantime ordered his charger, upon which he rode at the battle of Minden, to be fully caparisoned, and dressed himself in military costume. With pistol and sword in hand he mounted the courser, and commanding the stable-yard gates to be opened, rode among the multitude, who, astonished at any resistance, were immediately stricken with fear, and, dreading an attack from the terrible figure on horseback, as he was afterwards described to be, without staying to look behind, but using their legs with their utmost strength and diligence, made their way homeward, many declaring they thought they heard him at their heels the whole of the way. Enough were found, when a leader was presented, to capture the ringleaders of the mob : resistance was out of the question, and order was immediately restored ; a few of the most disorderly were punished, and no attempt was again made against the new regulation. A small company of men, selected from the estate and neighbourhood, was about this time raised by the duke, and put under the direction of captain Smyth. They were regularly exercised for some time on Sunday mornings, before the house, and their arms placed in the porter's lodge, where they still remain.

then placed here, secured within netted compartments; a dove-house, and conveniences for rearing and keeping poultry were made, and a family was placed in the dwelling called the BIRD HOUSE, to whose custody the whole was committed.

From the Bird-house, and leaving the large kitchen-garden to the left, a broad avenue, principally of beech, ascends gently to the extreme south-west point of the park, from whence bursts immediately on the sight a wide extent of scenery, which it would be useless for a common pen to attempt to describe. It is said to be bounded on the east by the Dover cliffs, and by the coast of Hampshire on the west; exhibiting almost the whole of the weald of Kent, and a great portion of the northern part of Sussex. It presents a charming variety of surface, the colouring changing with the time of day, and the effect of sun and shade: the long masses of forest and park foliage, here lit up by a sudden gleam, and there lying in the grey obscurity which a passing cloud throws over them: the horizon, though extremely delicate in its distant tints, one moment clearly defined against the sky, then gradually lost as a far-off shower draws before it its misty veil, and again breaking forth as we watch the watery curtain travelling on over the long tract of country.

Some few spots in the picture possess a charm distinct from either form or colour; and many there are who will pardon us for staying to point to them. Nearly in the centre appear the now desolate park and grounds of Penshurst, the cradle and the tomb of the Sidneys; a little higher up are the battlements of Eridge, once a hunting-seat of Warwick's great earl, now the residence of the earl of Abergavenny; more to the right, and skirting the horizon, is Ashdown Forest, a part of which may be readily recognized by a solitary clump of trees, upon a considerable convexity, apparently bare and uncultivated, known by the name of Gill's Lap, which, with the surrounding lands, formed part of the ancient domains of the Sackvilles, long before and subsequent to their elevation to the peerage. Between this and Boar Place, in Whitley Forest (the ancient seat of the Willoughbys and Hydes), may be distinctly seen Hever Castle, once the residence of Anne Boleyn, and afterwards of the unfortunate Anne of Cleves. A memento of the turbulence and power of the barons of old, is visible in the remains of the castle of Tunbridge, once a strong hold of the powerful earls of Clare.

Many objects of interest here present themselves; but we grow tiresome, and must pass on. The church-tower of Goudhurst, however, placed so conspicuously, and others whose vanes shoot up between the tufted clumps toward the Sussex hills, bring to the recollection two sources of present comfort and opulence, which, although so very differently located in the present day, were here originally planted; we advert to the woollen manufactures and casting of iron,—the art of weaving broad cloth being unknown in England, before its introduction by foreign refugees, and their settlement in the first mentioned place, and the adjoining towns; and the Sussex foundries supplying no inconsiderable part of the demand for that description of articles in use in their day.  The spires also of Wadhurst, Rotherfield, and Mayfield, once friendly guides to the bewildered traveller, forcibly call to remembrance the danger of the foul ways through the Weald, which, in the fourteenth century, caused the death of an archbishop.  The excellent roads, which may now be traced running far among well-cultivated fields, the rich orchards and hop-grounds, and the numberless mansions which peep forth from the groves by which they are nearly surrounded, strikingly contrast with the former state of the whole.

A sharp descent brings us from this mount into a broad valley, sweeping around almost the whole of the park, the banks of which are hung with trees of nearly every description of foliage; in one part excluding all other objects; in another, opening to permit us to catch the gateway-towers of the house, rising picturesquely on the hill above; and again in others allowing a glance up long shady vistas of stems, between which the deer swiftly bound, and where the sun-light, breaking through the dense leafy covering, falls on them as they pass, and on the rich velvet of the mossy sward. Pleasant it is in these glades, in the quiet evening, as the gloom steals on, and we lose the outlines even of the trunks whose light bark flashed so brightly in the gay sun, to listen to the unearthly whispers of the night breeze coming from afar, to hear it stirring the branches high above, and to trace the last sigh dying away among the distant groves, as the deep stillness returns. Cold indeed must be the heart which can feel none of the sweet influences of this park's delightful scenery,—which is neither moved by its present beauties, nor its interesting memorials of the past.

# THE MANSION.

The approach to the mansion from the town of Sevenoaks (distant from London about twenty-four miles) is through an entrance gate, nearly opposite the church, from which an avenue descends to the valley where the park is entered by its principal gate between two lodges. The road then crosses the valley, and, turning to the left, by a broad sweep ascends a hill beautifully covered with splendid forest trees, which prevent a distant view of Knole. From the foot of the hill, by inclining gently to the right, a path leads more directly to the house; and on surmounting the steep ascent, a front view of it, as represented in the frontispiece, breaks on the sight. The road formerly passed between two fine sycamore trees, the largest of which, remarkable for its

its size and beauty, was blown down a few years since, and, being a favourite tree, several articles of furniture for the house (among others the dining-room tables) were made from it. Near it was to be seen, securely fixed in the ground to a stake, a ring used for bull-baiting, to which there was formerly great resort in duke Lionel's time.

This magnificent seat is at present occupied by Mary, countess-dowager of Plymouth, relict of the late Other Archer, sixth earl of Plymouth, and eldest daughter of the late John Frederick, third duke of Dorset. Her ladyship now constantly resides here; notwithstanding which, every facility is afforded by her to gratify the curiosity of all respectable applicants to view the state-rooms of the mansion and their treasures of art—an indulgence to the public kindly continued by her ladyship, in imitation of the liberality of her noble ancestors.

The principal parts of this antique edifice form a spacious quadrangle, chiefly in the

M

castellated style, with several square towers and two large embattled gateways. At the rear, are numerous other smaller buildings, of very irregular character. The whole pile is estimated to occupy an area of three acres and a quarter; an extent which, combined with the feudal aspect of the chief portion of the structure, very forcibly directs the imagination to the distant days of baronial splendour,

" And pomp, and feast, and revelry."

The front of the mansion is in the plain style of the Elizabethan age, or that of her immediate successor, and has an air of unaffected simplicity.

The entrance is through a lofty embattled gateway, having towers at each angle, attached to which on either side, are spacious wings, pierced with three tiers of windows, each divided into three lights, by stone mullions, the upper tier being inserted in gables of a fanciful shape, and forming the attic story. Between these gables, and on their angular projections, are obelisk-shaped embellishments, the apex being crowned with a leopard sejant, supporting a shield of Sackville; which may also be found on many parts of the building, interior as well as exterior.

Concerning the dates of the several parts of this extensive pile, it is now impossible to give any certain account. There is reason to believe that there was an edifice on this spot so early as the time of the Normans; but it may be boldly stated, that nothing now remains which can be assigned to the architecture of that period.

The author of " Biographical Sketches,"* published in 1795, says, " the architecture bespeaks a variety of dates. The most ancient parts are probably coeval with the Mareschals and Bigods [See POSSESSORS OF KNOLE, p. 2]; and it seems as if the whole of it was antecedent to its becoming the possession of the Sackvilles, though many of this family have considerably re-

* " Biographical Sketches of Eminent Persons," 8vo. pp. 164, a compilation said to have been written by Henry Norton Willis, Esq.

paired it." We confess it would be out of our power to point out any portion of this building which can be referred to so early a period as the commencement of the thirteenth century (the time of the Mareschals and Bigods), and believe, that on the most careful survey, such a supposition will be rejected. The style of the different parts of this building is certainly remarkably various; many portions being very rude, and others exhibiting undoubted traits of architectural beauty and good design. But, though the parts on examination are heterogeneous, the pile, viewed as a whole, has an air of primitive grandeur which is exceedingly imposing. This arises partly from the fact, that whatever doubt may exist concerning the æra of the earliest portion of the mansion, the date of the *latest* is certain;—its external form or character has not been altered *since* the first year of the reign of James I. (1603-4), when the celebrated lord Buckhurst,* then created earl of Dorset,

---

* See a notice of this nobleman, p. 23.

first came to reside here; and probably it
had been then untouched for many years:
and with regard to the *oldest* portion, it is
stated in an old "Topographical Survey of
Kent," by Richard Kilburne, of Hawkherst, published in 1659, that Archbishop
Bourchier "*rebuilt* the manor-house, in-
closed a parke round the same, and resided
much at it." Mr. Hasted, in his "History
of Kent" (folio, 1778), repeats this statement, on Kilburne's authority; and further
quotes an indenture, dated June 30, 1457,
by which lord Say and Sele sold to the
archbishop, together with the manor, &c. of
Knole, (see ante, page 6), "all the tymbre,
wood, ledde, stone, and breeke, lying within
the said manor, at the quarrie of John
Cartiers, in the parish of Seale," which was
probably intended by his lordship for the
rebuilding of the mansion, and used by the
archbishop for that purpose. If these authorities might be relied on, and we may be
permitted to understand the word "rebuilt"
in its literal signification, the date of the
*oldest* portion of Knole House might be pre-

sumed to be 1457, or somewhat later, and that of its *most* recent portion, 1603-4, or thereabouts.

This, however, may be objected to from the following considerations. That the second gateway-tower, and the portion of the building immediately connected with it, will, on examination, appear to have received several alterations; and therefore will rather seem to have been adapted by the archbishop to his purpose, than wholly erected by him. An inspection of the oriel window (an engraving of which with the tower is here given) will shew that it is inserted in a wall which must have been of earlier construction, the heads of some of the machicolations* being just visible above the frame-work of the window, so much of them only having been cut away as was necessary to allow the introduction of the

* Perpendicular holes or grooves left between the corbels of a parapet, in the inside the wall, for the purpose of throwing down stones, or pouring molten lead, &c., on the heads of assailants: they are usually over the gateway only.

new work, and these openings probably
being considered no longer requisite. The
window and machicolations would hardly
have been built at the same time, as the
former, by its projection, would have rendered annoyance from above impossible,
except at the sides, the oriel forming a protection over the centre of the gateway.

The style of the window we presume to
be that of the time of Archbishop Bourchier, and his cognizance still being in the
glass, strengthens this supposition. There
are also internal evidences of a regard to
caution, in the construction of some original
openings still apparent, which would have
been useless, had windows of the size and
occupying the position of the present, been
a part of the original design.

That side of the house known by the
name of "lord George's side" appears also
to have undergone considerable alteration;
it has at present no direct internal communication with the house, and an inspection
of the roof from within, presents an appearance of adaptation not originally contem-

plated. In this roof there are three fine
ornamented tie-beams, or girders, having
the under part worked into a flat-pointed
arch with pierced spandrils, and some fram-
ing of open work attached to the upper
part of each end, which was formerly continued farther.

That these beams were a part of an open
ornamented timbered roof belonging to a
room of considerable size, forming a portion
of the mansion at a very early period, is not
improbable, as such roofs are still to be
found in some ancient halls which continue
in their original state. The relative position of the roof in which these girders are
found, to that of the kitchen, is also quite
in accordance with many ancient examples;
as the former, if continued, would present
nearly a straight line with the latter; and
the entrance to the kitchen from the hall,
could then have been immediately under the
screen, thus allowing that direct communication between the two apartments, so necessary when their original relations to each
other are considered. May we not, therefore,

conclude this to have been the direction and scite of the ancient great hall, which could have been approached by the gateway; moreover, many great halls being built upon a crypt, this also would have had the only existing cellar in the house for its foundation.

The ancient kitchen at Knole, a very large building still in use, is generally supposed to have been a part of the archbishop's erections here: it has a pointed roof, two immense fire-places, and windows opening inwards, from the rooms belonging to the cook and the comptroller of the kitchen. The present great hall is generally allowed to be the work of Thomas, first earl of Dorset, and, not quite agreeing with the site of the kitchen (although quite conformable to many examples in the relation of its position to the arch of entrance), certainly appears to be a deviation from the original plan.

The door of communication between the present hall and kitchen, is not original; the ancient appearance of this end of the

N

building being quite destroyed. But an old shelf is still left, with its huge knocker, for announcing to the guests that the preparations for the meal were completed, and that it was about to be removed to the board. A row of hatches, above the shelf, was remaining as late as 1790.

If the above suppositions be correct, we must assign a much earlier date to some parts of the building than that before-mentioned.* But, whatever may be the real dates of the erection of the numerous and multiform buildings which collectively constitute Knole House, the visitor who approaches the place expecting to be gratified with a view of fine architecture, will be disappointed. It is the extent of the pile, the incongruity of its several parts, the extraordinary number and apparent inutility of its rooms, galleries and staircases, which will first arrest the attention. It is plain that these appendages

* These remarks are submitted to the reader by W. E., with great diffidence, after a long acquaintance with the locality, from an unwillingness to allow an opportunity to pass for vindicating the antiquity of these remains.

of grandeur are now of little use even to
their proprietors, except to invest them with
the pleasing power of gratifying their less
affluent contemporaries; and, reflecting on
the uses for which they were originally
built and employed, we recollect that "the
times are altered," and that these remnants
of ancient English magnificence are, like
many other things, no longer applicable to
their original purpose.

Knole was built for a mode of life utterly
at variance with modern habits; in the days
when "barons bold" kept up a system of
hospitality and pomp, with costly retinues,
involving the feeding and lodging of numbers. To maintain such a system, the hall,
which was destined to be the chief scene of
festive enjoyment, was necessarily spacious;
the drawing-room and dining-room were
also handsome apartments; and there might
be two or three others; but the rest of the
house generally consisted of a vast number of comparatively small rooms, for the
accommodation of retainers and visitors,
many of them built from time to time, as

they were wanted, and grafted in a very
awkward manner on the main edifice.

These remarks are not peculiarly applicable to Knole, though they strictly apply
to that mansion, as well as to others of the
same age; neither are they expressed in
disparagement of that or any other structure; for, the very circumstances that we
have referred to, afford pleasing illustration
of the customs of former times, and the
genuine character of the details of Knole
House will more than compensate for their
want of systematic beauty, or architectural
uniformity.

A stanza from Lord Byron, in which he
depicts an English mansion under the disguised name of "Norman Abbey," may be
quoted as accurately descriptive of Knole
House:—

"Huge hall, long galleries, spacious chambers, joined
By no quite lawful marriage of the arts,
Might shock a connoisseur; but when combined,
Form a whole which, irregular in parts,
Yet leaves a grand impression on the mind;
At least of those whose eyes are in their hearts."

Don Juan, Canto XIII. s. 67.

What parts of the edifice were built by archbishop Bourchier; what were added by his successors, Moreton and Warham (see page 6); and what alterations and additions were made by the first earl of Dorset, and the successive earls and dukes of that noble house, are points of inquiry, which to the antiquary would prove highly interesting; but as we do not ourselves profess to be competent to enter the lists on such learned and debateable ground, where it must be admitted that proofs are slight, and much must rest on plausible conjecture; and, as we believe that the majority of our readers will joyfully dispense with elaborate discussion; we must content ourselves with "generalities," and state, as a mere hint to the curious, that it is believed that the old house, previously to archbishop Bourchier's time, occupied principally the site of the north-east end and its offices. This portion appears to have been burnt down on Shrove-Sunday, 1623: many of its windows are evidently of about that date; and it is probable that the greater part of the north-east end (except the wall, which is certainly more ancient) was destroyed, and subsequently rebuilt. For the rest of the edifice, the whole, except the front, has been generally considered to have been rebuilt by archbishop Bourchier, about the year 1457. The front, including the porter's lodge, &c., is supposed to have been added by archbishop Moreton, between the years 1486 and 1500; add to which, that very essential repairs and alterations were most probably made by the first earl of Dorset.*

It is not, however, to criticise the details

---

* The author does not pretend to be versed in architectural antiquities; and it should therefore be mentioned, that these remarks on the architecture of Knole House are offered, with a full consciousness of his own insufficiency, as the result of his (unskilled) personal observation during a brief residence on the spot. Books will not aid the enquiry: at least the author has referred in vain to Hasted's Kent, and other histories of the county, to Neale's "Seats," Hills "Munimenta Antiqua," Amsinck's "Tunbridge Wells," "Vitruvius Britannicus," Britton and Brayley's "England and Wales," Lewis, Capper, and Gorton's "Topographical Dictionaries," &c. &c.

of its architecture, that the majority of
visitors approach Knole House; though we
doubt not that both information and amusement might be derived from such an object.
But, to the ordinary visitor, this mansion
offers other and very powerful attractions,
in its galleries of art, containing many of
those great creations of the pencil which
are " of all time," and excite at once wonder
and delight, and in its numerous relics of
ancient magnificence, which afford a pleasing illustration of the domestic decorations,
manners and customs of our ancestors.
The pictures are of course not of equal
merit; but several might be mentioned,
the view of any *one* of which would amply
repay the connoisseur for visiting the place;
and the collection is particularly rich in
portraits of eminent characters, which are
both abundant and in good preservation.
The apartments are of themselves a memo-
rial of obsolete grandeur, and their splendid
old-fashioned furniture affords a very perfect specimen of the style which prevailed
in the reigns of Elizabeth and James I.

These are the "sights" at Knole, for which most persons will be content to forego antiquarian disquisitions. Yet, we must impress on our readers that the building itself, on every side, is worth many a passing glance, and eminently calculated to excite sentiments of veneration: for who can contemplate the present magnitude of the building, and its feudal style, without suffering the memory to revert to by-gone ages, and the mind to re-people the past with knights, ecclesiastics, statesmen, and princely nobles—the Says, the Cranmers, the Sackvilles, and others, associated by history or tradition with this ancient domain? The very exterior inspires these pleasing visions, and the charm becomes still stronger when we cross the antique quadrangles, and enter the splendid Gothic hall, with its massive and richly-carved music-gallery, its dais, or raised floor, for the lord's seat, its long oak-table for the tenantry and retainers, its painted glass, and its noble proportions. Immersed in thought, we feel ourselves carried back some centuries, until awakened from our reverie by a smartly-dressed modern porter, or domestic, flitting before our eyes, or by an intimation from the courteous house-keeper that we may "follow her." The illusion vanishes; we perceive where we are, recollect for what purpose, and by whose indulgence, we have been admitted, and look forward as "beings of to-day" to the real treat which awaits us, the details of which are given with scrupulous minute-ness in the following pages.

Settee in the Leicester Gallery.

## THE ROOMS SHEWN TO VISITORS; WITH CATALOGUES OF THE PICTURES, &c.

THE entrance into the mansion is through the front tower-portal; over the gateway of which will be observed two escutcheons, the one bearing the arms of Sackville, the other those of Cranfield; supposed to have been placed here in the time of the fifth earl, whose countess was the daughter of Lionel Cranfield, earl of Middlesex. Passing the porter's lodge, which contains a small number of muskets, and some ancient halberts, the visitor enters the first or green court, a quadrangle, with a grass plot on either side of the pathway through it; that on the right being ornamented with a cast of the celebrated statue, known as the *Gladiator repellens*, and that on the left, with one of *Venus*, as rising from the bath. Over the gateway, and in the range of buildings on each side of it, are numerous apartments, few of which, except some on the ground floor, are ever used, unless as repositories for old furniture, &c. Among these rooms, is a suite known as lord John's, from their having been formerly occupied by that nobleman, who was the second son of Lionel, duke of Dorset, and father of John-Frederick, the third duke.

From the first quadrangle, the entrance into the second or stone court is through a gateway, having a machicolated parapet, below which, and immediately over the arch, is a fine oriel window (an engraving of which has already been given.) Before passing on, the curious observer will notice the site of a loop-hole in a projection of

the wall close to his elbow on the left hand
side, through which the cautious warder
might scrutinize his visitors before admit-
ting them.  The archway is groined, and has,
at the intersections of the cross-springers,
openings for the annoyance of an enemy.

In the room over this archway (which is
not, however, shewn to visitors) are two
corbels of stone, each bearing a shield, one
inscribed with the word 𝕸𝖊𝖗𝖈𝖞, within a
knot, and the other having the letters 𝖙𝖍𝖈
within a double triangle.  The approaches
to this room are by two massive oaken
doors, of the rudest workmanship, and
strongly studded with iron.  To the window
(the oriel) is an ascent of two steps, and
there, still preserved in a quatrefoil com-
partment, painted on the glass, is a falcon
rising, between two Bourchier's knots.

At the further side of the stone court now
entered, is a portico supported by eight
Ionic columns, over which is an open gallery with a balustrade for walking; and surmounting the parapet above is a fine stone
shield, bearing the arms and quarterings of

Cranfield, removed from Copthall, when
that ancient mansion was taken down. Over
doorways at each end of the portico are
busts of king William III., and in the centre
is an allegorical carving fixed in the wall
between the attires of a moz-deer which
were found in a marl-pit near the moun-
tains of Wicklow, in Ireland, and presented
by a Mr. Brown to Lionel, duke of Dorset.
There are also some fine specimens of the
horns of British deer. Inserted in the walls
of this court are some small pieces of antique
sculpture, chiefly fragments, with inscrip-
tions, brought from the continent with other
remains, about twenty years since, some
of which are preserved in like manner in
the garden front. The whole area of this
court was excavated a few years since, to
form a reservoir for collecting the rain-
water which falls upon the roofs, thus insuring an abundant supply.

Two doors on the left hand of the arch of
entrance from this stone court to the hall,
belong to apartments formerly used for
the delivery of provisions, no person being

allowed to enter except the peculiar officer, who placed the articles required on a shelf which crossed the door immediately below hatches made for that purpose.

Visiting the apartments in the order in which they are shewn, we enter

## THE GREAT HALL,

N apartment of noble dimensions, finely proportioned, and in a good style of architecture, with tesselated pavement (much worn). It measures seventy-four feet ten inches in length, twenty-seven in breadth, and twenty-six feet eight inches in height, and is built after the plan of the Anglo-Normans, having the *dais*, or raised floor at one end of it, agreeably to ancient usage, for the principal table for the noble possessor of the mansion; while other tables stood lengthwise down the hall, for the use of visitors, tenants, or domestics: A table of this latter kind is preserved here : it is of oak, and is constructed for the once-popular game of shuffle-board.

In the windows are some armorial bearings in stained glass ; among others, the royal arms of Elizabeth, with supporters, and the arms of Robert Devereux, earl of Essex.

In the fire-place is a curious pair of fire-irons or dogs : on one are the arms of Henry VIII, surmounted with a crown, and the initials H. R.; on the other, a falcon crowned standing on the stump of a tree, from which issue the white and red roses, (a cognizance of Anne Boleyn,) with the initials H. A., as seen in the engraving. They were purchased at a sale at Hever Castle in Kent, formerly the residence of Sir Thomas Boleyn, her father.

The hall is separated from the passage by an oaken screen, enclosing a music gallery boldly carved. Among the quaint architectural enrichments with which it is decorated, the heraldic cognizances* of the family stand prominent, and shields charged with the coats of Sackville and Baker (those of Thomas, first earl of Dorset, and his countess) establish the date of its erection. Towards the top there is a row of small latticed windows, and the whole is finished by the arms, supporters, and other ornaments belonging to the house of Dorset.

The walls are ornamented with the following pictures:

1. First earl of Middlesex, full-length, artist not known.
2. Third earl of Dorset    .   ditto
3. Countess of Monmouth    ditto

* These cognizances are, a black ram's head; a white leopard rampant, pellette; the same sejant, holding a shield of Sackville; and a demi-red dragon, rising from the waves.

4. Edward, fourth Earl of Dorset, half-length.

5. George III, and Queen Charlotte, full-length—*Ramsay*.

6. View of, and procession to Dover Castle, in which are introduced the portraits of Lionel, duke of Dorset, Sir Basil Dixon, Maximilian Buck, chaplain to his grace, and many years rector of Kemsing and Seale, and some others.—*Wotton*. A large and clever picture, 10 feet by 7.

7. Lord Buckhurst and Lady M. Sackville, full-lengths.—*Kneller*.

8. A Boar-hunt—*F. De Vos*. A fine picture, boldly painted; the pencilling free and characteristic.

9. Death of Marc Antony, 7 feet 9 inches, by 5 feet 4 inches.—*Dance*.

10. The Finding of Moses.—*Giordano*.

11. *John, Lord Somers*. (1.)*—Kneller.

12. Silenus and Bacchanals, 6 feet 4 inches

* When figures between parentheses occur after the name of a portrait is given, reference is made to the Appendix. This will apply throughout the rooms.

P

by 5 feet 11 inches.—*Rubens.*  A fine
picture, deemed one of the artist's most
powerful works.

13. *Lady Shannon.*—Kneller.

The statues are :—

*Perseus, with the head of Medusa.*  A
plaister after Canova.

*Demosthenes delivering an oration.*— A
Grecian statue, in marble, the size of life,
purchased in Italy by the third duke of
Dorset for £700.   It is a fine composition;
but the figure being in the attitude of calm
discussion, and its most marked character
being that of deliberative composure, it has
been doubted whether it is rightly named.
The duke presented a cast of this statue to
the Royal Academy, and there, it is worthy
of notice, it is entitled *Pythagoras.*

*The goddess Egeria*—a recumbent female
figure, in marble, on a wooden pedestal;
considered to have been a goddess who
presided over child-birth, as the Juno-
Lucina of the Romans.

Three small marble figures, supposed to
represent the Seasons; and some others;

among the rest an equestrian statue of Julius Cæsar, and a bust of the poet Prior.

Quitting the hall, the visitor ascends to the other apartments by the principal staircase (of which our artist has endeavoured to convey some idea in the illustration which faces this page,) the passage to which is painted in two colours, with a fanciful combination of scrolls, animals, and foliage, nearly fac-similes of the designs used to ornament the principal chapters of the embellished folios of the time of Elizabeth and James I., and the walls of the staircase having, also, in panels, various conversational and emblematic subjects, in keeping with the surrounding decorations. In the glass are a shield exhibiting the alliances of the house, and horizontal rows of small quarries, bearing the family crests. One of the standards supporting the hand-rail, and crowned with the leopard sejant affronté, terminates below in a group of cockatrices fancifully combined.

The ancient lantern depending from the ceiling is worthy of notice from the homely contrivance exhibited for adjusting its elevation.

On arriving at the top of the staircase
the first room entered is

## THE BROWN GALLERY.

AN interesting apart-
ment, eighty-eight feet
in length, with floor
and sides of oak, (the
latter in panels), and
the hinges and fasten-
ings of the doors made
of iron, curiously orna-
mented and kept bright. The ceiling is
of an elliptic form, divided into compartments by oaken fret-work, which imparts a
sombre yet pleasing appearance to the
whole.

In the windows are a shield containing
France and England within the Garter,
very old; a fleur-de-lis, and a double rose,
each surrounded by a garland, and ensigned
with a royal crown; and three ostrich feathers, enclosed in a garland and surmounted
by a large coronet of beautiful shape and

elaborate pattern, belonging to the princes of the blood royal: the quill of each of these feathers is charged with three bezants, and an escrol, inscribed " Ich Dien," passes in front of the bottom of them, but is not transfixed by the ends of 'either. Much has been written on differences found upon the feathers, which are well known to be very significant, but these roundles have hitherto escaped notice, which induces an enquiry into their meaning. The feather, we are told, was borne by all the sons of Edward III, and is mentioned as belonging to the monarch himself; but it was then borne singly, the quill or pen thereof being tinctured for difference; thus, the king's feather was argent, with the quill gold; the prince's quill and feather both silver; the duke of Lancaster's feather silver, quill ermine; and the duke of Somerset's compony, blue and silver. It is farther stated, that the feathers were never used as a plume by any of the princes of Wales, till the time of Henry VII, when they first so appear upon the sepulchral chapel of prince Arthur,

where they also occur singly among other
badges. As a difference from the royal
arms, the dukes of York used a label, each
point charged with three torteaux (round
red spots), which also appeared upon the
supporters and crest. May we not be
allowed to suppose that Henry Tudor, when
duke of York, charged the quill of his feather with the same difference as appeared
upon his label, following the examples of
the dukes of Lancaster and Somerset? Or
did he, upon his being created prince of
Wales, after his brother Arthur's death,
place upon the prince's badge, his own
peculiar difference, thus shewing himself to
be at once prince of Wales and duke of
York? In reply to an objection, which
might be raised from the colour of these
roundles being yellow, while those used by
the dukes of York were red, it may be
stated that such differences are not uncommon in old stained glass, owing to mecha-
nical accidents.

A superb collection of portraits, many of
them of persons of the highest celebrity in

English history, now claims the attention of the visitor. By whom they were all painted is unknown; some of them certainly by Holbein, and most of them, probably, by his pupils. Among them are many of the principal nobles and statesmen who lived in the reigns of Henry VIII., Mary, Elizabeth, and James. The entire collection is in excellent preservation, but the authenticity of some of the portraits is questionable, and the majority of them are clearly copies. Those in the following catalogue which are printed in italics, may be particularly noticed as works of art.

1. *Oliver Cromwell.*—Walker. A clever picture, painted with force and freedom, but somewhat differing from the usual prints and paintings of the Protector.

2. Edward, fourth Earl of Dorset.—A copy.

3. The Poet (Dryden).—A copy.

4. Representation of a Masked Ball, given by Cardinal Wolsey to King Henry VIII. and Anne Boleyn. A curious

picture, but coarse, said to be by *Tintoretti.*

5. *A Bacchanalian Scene.*—Hemskirk. A humorous subject, carefully finished, with the truth of colour, and natural familiar air, of the Flemish school.

6. A Battle-piece.—A copy.

7. Alphonso D'Avalos, Marquis de Guasto, Lieutenant-General of the armies of the Emperor Charles V. in Italy: he died in 1546, æt. 42.

8. Don John of Austria (2).

9. The Duke of Parma (3).

10. Henry of Lorraine, Duc de Guise (4).

11. Charles, Duc de Bourbon, Constable of France (5).

12. Ann de Montmorenci, Peer, Marshal and Constable of France (6).

13. Henry Howard, Earl of Northampton (7).

14. Francis, Duc de Guise (8).

15. Herbert, Earl of Pembroke (9).

16. Dudley, Duke of Northumberland (10).

17. Friar Bacon (11).

18. John Wickliffe, the Reformer (12).

Gardiner, Bishop of Winchester, &c. (13).

Sir James Wilford (14).

Queen Mary.

George Clifford, Earl of Cumberland (15).

Fisher, Bishop of Rochester (16).

Cranmer, Archbishop of Canterbury (17)

Cromwell, Earl of Essex (18)

The Earl of Surrey; supposed the Earl of Surrey beheaded by Henry VIII.

Sir Thomas More (19).

Thomas Howard, Duke of Norfolk (20).

King Henry VIII.

Henry Fitz-Alan, Earl of Arundel (21).

Cardinal Wolsey (22).

Whitgift, Archbishop of Canterbury (23).

Sir Francis Walsingham (24).

Egerton, Baron Ellesmere (25).

Lord Burleigh (26).

Sir Christopher Hatton (27).

*Queen Elizabeth.* Remarkable for the elaborate profusion of drapery, and the singular manner in which it is disposed. The tints of the face appear much faded.

Q

38. Dudley, Earl of Leicester (28).
39. Thomas Sackville, first Earl of Dorset. The Lord Buckhurst of Queen Elizabeth's court.
40. Charles Howard, Earl of Nottingham (29).
41. Cecil, Earl of Salisbury (30).
42. Sir Francis Drake (31).
43. Howard, Earl of Suffolk (32).
44. Admiral Blake (33).
45. Sir John Norris (34).
46. Bancroft, Archbishop of Canterbury, (35).
47. William, first Prince of Orange (36).
48. Ratcliff, Earl of Sussex (37).
49. King James I.
50. Sir Walter Mildmay (38.)
51. Queen Jane Seymour.
52. *Queen Katharine.*—Holbein.
53. Sir Thomas More (19.
54. Not known.
55. *Isabella Clara Eugenia*, Governess of the Low Countries (40). A very clever, well-finished picture.
56, 7, 8 & 9. Not known.

60. Erasmus (39).
61. *Early Reformers;* viz. Martin Luther (47), Melancthon, and Pomeranus, (41).
62. Agricola (42).
63. Huss, the Reformer (43).
64. *Milton*, the poet.—A pleasing portrait; expressive, mild, and dignified.
65, 6, 7 & 8. Four small pictures of the Seasons.
69. French painting of Scenery.
70. *A Florentine Nobleman*, supposed of the Strozzi family. This picture is generally much admired.
71. A Lady (not known).
72. *St. John and Lamb.*—Dominichino. A sweet picture, but more in the style of Correggio.
73. Isabella Bonotta, Countess de Mori.
74. Not known.
75. Baron Montmorenci.
76. The Duc D'Alvarez (44).
77. Not known.
78. *Ninon de L'Enclos.*—Bromhino. A highly-finished likeness, said to have been painted at the age of 70 (45).
79. *The Countess of Desmond;* (46.) An inte-

resting portrait, and a characteristic, clear picture.

80. The Earl of Surrey; supposed Francis, first earl.

81. Martin Luther (47).

82. *Man in ruff* (not known). A painting of considerable merit; the features well expressed, the colouring good, and the touch decided and free.

83. King Edward VI.

84. Philip, Count de Horne (48).

85. Portrait (in oval frame); not known.

86. The Queen of Francis I.

87. Queen Ann Boleyn.

88. The Emperor Charles V.

89. *King Charles II.*—Sir P. Lely. Three-quarter length.

90. Portrait (half in armour); not known.

91. King Henry V.

92. Louis XV. Old print.

93. William, Prince of Orange.—*Jansen.*

94. James, second Earl of Middlesex.

95. A Doge of Venice.

96. Honourable Edward Cranfield.

97 & 98. Seventh Lord and Lady Abergavenny.

The chairs and other seats in this apartment are worthy of remark for antiquity,

shape, and material; velvets and silks of the finest texture and richest patterns (the colours of some in a remarkable state of preservation) cover a variety of curiously-formed frames, some high-backed and low-seated, others precisely the reverse, and others again softly cushioned up to the elbows, requiring a rather high stool for the feet, which is furnished in its place; these, together with ornamental furniture of corresponding date, give a high degree of interest and value to the whole; so great a variety of objects, agreeing in age and style with the apartment they furnish, being seldom met with.

## LADY BETTY GERMAINE'S BED-CHAMBER.

THE lady who gives name to this apartment lived in the reign of George II., and was a patroness of literature. She was daughter of the earl of Berkeley, and became the second wife of Sir John Germaine. Both died without issue, and by virtue of their wills,* lord George Sackville obtained an act of parliament to assume the surname of Germaine.

* Lady Betty Germaine died Dec. 16th, 1769. By her will left to lady Vere £20,000—to lord George Sackville £20,000, with Drayton House and the manor thereunto belonging—to lady Catherine Beauclerk £1,000, and her best diamond ring—to earl Berkeley a gold cup—to Mr. Berkeley £5,000—to the countess of Granard £5,000—to lady Craven £3,000—to lady Temple £500 for a ring;—her jewels, plate, &c. to be sold, and, with the residue of her estate, to be equally divided between lord and lady Vere and Sir George Sackville.

In this chamber is a piece of tapestry exhibiting portraits of the celebrated Vandyke, and his father-in-law, lord Gowrie.

The paintings here are—

The Earl of Halifax.

Edward, fourth Earl of Dorset.

*Cymon and Iphigenia* (over the mantelpiece).

A Moonlight.

Flemish Toper and Companion.

Judith with the head of Holofernes.

A Madonna.

An old Priest.

St. John preaching in the Wilderness.

An old painting (noticeable on account of its extraordinary disregard of perspective).

Banditti attacking Travellers.

*Holy Family* (ancient).

The artists are not known. The bedstead here is antique; it is of oak, with plumes and worked stuff furniture, lined with pink and fringed, and is covered with two or three curiously-embroidered counterpanes.

## LADY BETTY GERMAINE'S DRESSING ROOM.

A SMALL room, containing several articles of antique furniture, as carved stools, with crimson and damask covers, a japanned Indian table, &c.

The paintings are—

Mrs. Porter.—After *Lely*.

Elizabeth, first Duchess of Dorset.— *Hudson*.

*Lord Hunsdon.*—Holbein.

Thomas, first Earl of Dorset.

Robert, second Earl.

Cecile, first Countess.

Richard, third Earl.

Ann, third Countess.

Lady Margaret Sackville.

Marquess of Winchester.

A Holy Family.

Head of a Boy.

Triangular frame, containing three por-
traits of Kings of France.
*Nymphs and Echo.*—Lely.
The Lady of Sir Walter Raleigh.
Hunting Scene.
Miss Collier.—*Hudson.*
A Battle-piece.
*Mrs. Bates.*—Ozias Humphrey.
A Building in Rome.
King Lear and Ophelia.
Maurice, Prince of Orange.
Lord Leveson Gower.

## THE SPANGLED BED-ROOM.

THIS is a very hand-
some room, hung with
tapestry, and having an
original floor of oak,
which is painted black.
The furniture, too, is interesting, as illustrative
of the style of former
days: the whole of it (with the exception
of a Chinese or Indian idol, shrine and stand,

R

a gift of the present earl Amherst) was
presented by king James I. to Lionel, earl
of Middlesex, lord-treasurer, from whom it
descended, through his daughter, who married the fifth earl of Dorset, to the Sackville family.  The bed is very beautiful: it
has crimson silk furniture, lined with satin,
richly embroidered with gold and silver,
with coverlid to match.  There are also
several stools with crimson silk tops, embroidered after the same pattern; and a
curious antique ebony wardrobe merits
notice.  Here are two paintings only, portraits, but both fine ones, by Sir Peter
Lely; viz.

The Duke of Monmouth.

Mrs. Sackville.

## THE SPANGLED DRESSING-ROOM.

THIS also is an elegant apartment. In the centre of it stand a beautifully wrought chair and footstool of *ivory*, (also presented by earl Amherst, who brought them from India), in which, surrounded by the fine creations of the pencil which grace the walls, we should presume that a lady might sit with tolerable satisfaction during her toilet. There are some other handsome stools and settees, with crimson-damask covers, &c.; and the paintings are as follow :—

1. *A Miser,* with the Father of Evil at his elbow.—*Quintin Matsys.* A highly-finished and clever painting.
2. A Venus.—After *Titian.*
3. The Salutation.—*Rembrandt.*
4 & 5. *Candle-lights.*—Schalkchen. Delicately and elaborately finished, and generally attractive from their striking

effect, the peculiar tone of the light being given with great truth and force.

6. A frame containing six miniatures; viz. Lionel, first earl of Middlesex, Ann, Countess of Middlesex, Sir John Suckling, Mr. Brett, and two others.

7. Another frame, containing a miniature of Lady Rachel Fane, Countess of Bath and Middlesex.

8. A Sybil (Sybilla Persica).—*Stone.*

9. *Miss Stewart.*—Lely.

10. The Alchemyst.—*Wycke.*

11. *Ann Hyde, Duchess of York.*—Lely.

12. The Nativity.—*Bassano.*

13. *Venus and a Satyr.*—Correggio.

14. Robbers attacking a Waggon.—*Vandergucht.*

15. *Countess of Shrewsbury* (51).—Lely.

16. A Landscape.—*Salvator Rosa.*

17. Still Life.

18. *A Flemish Merry-making.*—Heemskirke.

19. A Reposing Venus.—*Ozias Humphrey.*

20. *James Compton, fifth Earl of Northampton.*—Vandyke.

21. Abraham entertaining the Angels.—
*Guercino.*

22. Lady Stafford.—*Albano.*

23. Lady Ossory.

24. *A Magdalene.*—Albano.

## THE BILLIARD-ROOM

 Is remarkable, not for its furniture, having little besides an old billiard-table, but for its pictures, several of which are undoubted originals, and most valuable.

1. St. Peter.—*Rembrandt.*

2. Old Man's Head; supposed Lord Sunderland.

3. Diana and Nymphs discovered by Actæon.—By or after *Titian.*

4. *Portrait of an Old Man.*—Bassano.

5. Sir Thomas More.—*Mytens.*

6. *Franks Hals*, by himself, in his peculiarly free and sketchy style.

7. Boy blowing a Pipe.—*Murillo.*

8 & 9. James, Lord Cranfield, and Lady Frances Cranfield (children of Lionel, Earl of Middlesex).—*Mytens.*

10. The God of Silence.

11. *Major Mohun* (52.)

12. *Sir Kenelm Digby* (53).—A splendid Vandyke; such a portrait as cannot fail to attract notice. The countenance is expressive and dignified—the colouring and execution admirable.

13. A Landscape.—*Poussin.*

14. Diana and Calisto.—After *Titian.*

15. *Du Bourg, Organist of Antwerp* (54).— Vandyke. Finely conceived and painted, full of poetical feeling, and possessing great interest.

16. A Landscape.—*Poussin.*

## THE LEICESTER GALLERY.

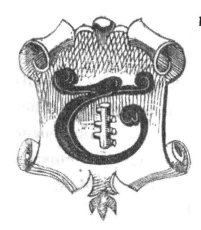

HIS apartment is ornamented throughout with fine paintings; its matting and screens are antique and curious, and with its sofas, couches, stools, &c. covered with crimson damask and figured velvet, it is highly illustrative of the style of the sixteenth century.

Two rolls of arms, displayed upon oaken stands, exhibit the Sackville and Curzon pedigrees. The former one in particular is an elaborate performance, and commences with Herbrand de Sackville, whose portrait appears in the window at one end of this gallery, finely executed on glass, with the following inscription : " 𝔥erbrandus de 𝔖ackbille, præpotens Normannus, intrabit Angliam cum Gulielmo Conquestore. A^no D^ni MLXVI." [Herbrand de Sackville, a very powerful

Norman, came into England with William the Conqueror, 1066.] This figure will bear the closest examination, and will be found to be exquisitely finished; the features and hands are correctly and carefully drawn, and the details of the armour and dress well made out. The pedigree is the work of Sir William Segar (Garter), Richard St. George (Norroy), and Henry St. George (Richmond), and was executed in the year 1623, in the time of Edward, the fourth earl.

The pictures in this room are—

1. *Countess of Bedford* (55)—Vandyke. A most captivating portrait; the drapery finely managed, and the hands exquisitely painted.

2. *A Landscape.*—Young artist from Rome.

3. *James, Marquess of Hamilton.*—Mytens. A fine full-length.

4. *Nicolo Molino, the Venetian Ambassador.*—Mytens. A full-length, also possessing great merit.

5. *Philip IV. of Spain.*—Sir Anto. Moore.

6. *Queen of Philip IV.*—Ditto.

7. Lady Milton.—*Pompeio Bottoni.*

8. Landscape.—Young artist from Rome.

9. Prince Henry, son of King James I., full-length.—*Mytens.*

10. King James I., at about the age of 60, sitting in a chair which is preserved in the Brown Gallery.—*Mytens.*

11. Sir Ralph Bosville (56).—*Schidoni.*

12. Duc D'Espernon.

13 & 16. Fruit pieces.

14 & 15. Landscapes.—*Deane.*

17. First Lord Whitworth and Nephew; three-quarter.

18 & 19. *Heraclitus* and *Democritus.*—Mignard. Amusing pictures, but coarsely painted.

20. Sir Hatton Fermor (57).

21. *First Earl of Middlesex.*—Mytens. A good portrait; the flesh tints are fine, the hands well disposed and painted, and the general effect pleasing.

22. *Henry Howard, Earl of Surrey* (58.)—Holbein.

23. Ann, Countess of Middlesex.—*Mytens.*

24. *Sir Anthony Cope* (59).—Vandyke.

s

25. Frederic, King of Bohemia.—*Houthoust.*
26. Princess Louise............. Ditto.
27. Portrait (not known).
28. King Charles II.—*Houthoust.*
29. Princess Sophia of Bohemia.—Ditto.
30. *Guardian Angel and Child.*—Cortona.
31. Edward, fourth Earl of Dorset.
32. A Sea-piece.—*Salvator Rosa.*

From the windows of these two rooms, which were formerly comprehended under the title of the Leicester Gallery, are views which deserve to be remarked, from their varied and peculiar character. The window in the billiard-room towards the north-east, overlooks the pleasure-grounds at the back of the house, and presents a fine variety of luxuriant evergreens, so characteristic of the ancient English mansion; behind which rise several lofty and picturesque firs. That at the farther end of the Leicester gallery commands a view of one of those ranges of chalk hills with which this part of Kent abounds, a portion of the park, with its clumps of trees and herds of deer; while immediately below is the building which formerly served as a prison to the mansion; and from a third we look down into a court-yard, surrounded by antique windows and gables.

## THE VENETIAN BED-ROOM.

This chamber received its designation from having been slept in by Nicolo Molino, the Venetian ambassador. It contains a very elegant state bed, said to have been prepared for the reception of king James II. The canopy is richly carved and gilt at the head-board, surmounted with the royal arms.

The furniture is of green cut-velvet, lined with lutestring; and the chairs and stools in the room are covered to correspond.

There are many other curious ornaments, &c.; but only three pictures, and of those, only one worthy of notice; namely—

Katherine II., of Russia, in military costume, as a commander-in-chief. (61).

Chair in the Venetian Bed-room.

## THE VENETIAN DRESSING-ROOM.

A SMALL carpet on the floor of this room, wrought with the arms of Curzon and Leveson, brings to mind Mr. Fosbroke's description: " In the sixteenth century we find carpets of English work, with arms in the centre, a square bord carpet cloth for the table, with arms in the midst of it, one large carpet for a coobard, Turkey carpets for the table, &c."

Here are many clever paintings; viz.

1. Lionel, first Duke of Dorset, on horseback.—*Wootton.*

2. *Sir Thomas More* (19).—Holbein.

3. Old Man's Head.   A fine study.

4. *A Boar-hunt.*   A very clever bit, though slight; said to be by Rubens.

5. *Miss Axford*, the fair Quakeress (62).— Sir Joshua Reynolds. This portrait, and

those of the opera-singer and opera-dancer (Nos. 6 & 14), all by Reynolds, are in that celebrated artist's usual broad and happy style, remarkable for sweetness of expression, and for admirable faithfulness to nature.

6. *Madame Baccelli*, an opera-dancer.—Sir Joshua Reynolds.

7. *Landscape.*—Berghem.

8. *Jacob's Journey.*—Bassano. .

9. Lady Hume.

10. Honourable Lionel Cranfield.

11. A Candlelight.

12. A Firelight.

13. Ann, Countess of Dorset, Pembroke, and Montgomery (63).—*Mytens.*

14. *Signora Schielleni*, an opera-singer.—Sir Joshua Reynolds.

15. *The Earl of Shaftesbury* (60).—Riley.

16. A Head, supposed of Cleopatra.

17. *A Toper.*

18. Old Man's Head.

19. *Monsieur Campchinetze* (65).—Gainsborough. An unassuming, but most clever picture.

20. Companion to the Toper.
21. *A Battle-piece.*—Borgognone. The hurry and confusion of the conflict are depicted with a bold and spirited pencil.
22. The Finding of Moses.—*Lairesse.*
23 & 24. Small portraits of Philip IV. of Spain, and his Queen.
25. *Landscape.*—Salvator Rosa.
26. *Death of Cleopatra.*—Dominichino.
27. Wife of Titian going to poison his mistress.—After *Titian.*
28. Repose, with Flight into Egypt.—*Zuccharelli.*
29. The Archduke Albert.
30. Isabella, Duchess of Brabant.
31. A Farm-yard.—*Honderkooter.*
32. Portrait of Mr. Brett.—*C. Jansen.*
33. Sir Kenelm Digby, half-length.—A copy.
34. *Mrs. Margaret Woffington* (the actress) *as Penelope.*—Sir J. Reynolds.
35. Ozias Humphrey.—By himself.

In the passage leading from the Leicester to the Brown gallery are several pictures,

as, the first Lord Whitworth, a Devotee, a
Garden-scene, Madonna and Child, and two
or three others; but none of any note.

## THE ORGAN ROOM.

 N ancient apartment of
extremely rude finish, the
walls being covered with
oak boards not framed
into paneling; but this
we may imagine to have
been remedied in the
olden time by the assist-
ance of the yeoman hanger with goodly
tapestries, of which there was great store,
of pattern and story most appropriate, the
floor being beseemly strewed with hay or
rushes, and the light of day softly beaming
through sacred scriptures, set forth by
goodly personages and most holy, in the
richly-coloured glass; thus, with its other
garniture, rendering it a chamber meet for
the most dainty player upon the organ
belonging to the chapel of the lord cardinal.

Add to these, the noble instrument* so con-
veniently placed that the organist could ob-
serve the altar below, assist with sweet music
at its service, and still remain unseen by those
engaged in it; while a small door near to a
fire-place, replenished with blazing logs if the
season so required, communicating immediately with the chapel, gave ready admittance
to those belonging to the choir, or others
whose business lay hither; for we should
not marvel if this may have been used as a
school for the nurture of those belonging to
the choir in the difficulties of their calling.
Upon the eve of great festivals we can
imagine from hence, much bustle and going
to and fro, very much care in the teacher,
and great pains taken by the scholar, in re-
citing the service that on the morrow was
by its grandeur to awaken the " Gloria in
excelsis Deo," and by its sweetness and
gentle harmony to impress on the heart
of both ecclesiastic and layman the conclu-

* Said to have been the second of the kind built in
England.

T

sion of the song " Et in terra pax, bene-
volentia ad hominem."

We may not here neglect the oaken chest,
so quaintly carved, whose fellow standeth
in the gate-house first entered, inasmuch as
the greybeards tell us (with what degree of
truth we know not) that it was a travelling-
box belonging to lord Buckhurst's brave
chariot, in which, drawn by a team of fine
oxen, he was used to journey so nobly to
and from the councils in which he was wont
to preside.

Among others, three pictures now remain
that of old were in the chapel. They appear to be the work of one hand, and done
to decorate the church or chapel of some religious fraternity, as may be seen by the
following inscription, placed at the corner of
one of them :—

> Ad Decorem Domus
> Dei. JOHANNES . AVYNGTON
> Doctor . et . SVBPRIOR
> me . FIERI . FECIT  Aᴼ D
> 1526 ET A . RE. H 8. 18.

The stories are—the Betrayal, the Resurrection, and the Ascension, painted in rich colours and overlaid in parts with gold: moreover, each tablet has depicted in two colours, on the other side, a saint in pontificalibus, with his name beneath in rubicund capitals, of ancient formation.

The paintings, most of which are but indifferent copies, are as follow :—

King James I.

A Musical Party.

Companion to ditto.

James Butler, Earl of Ormond.

Archbishop Bancroft (35) ; over the door.

Sir John Suckling.

Landscape, with figures.

Ditto, with building.

Charles, second Duke of Dorset, as a
    *Roman Emperor !*

Christ mocked (small).

Tobit and the Angel.

Dover Castle.

Charles I. and his Queen.

Sea-piece—story of Jonah.

## THE CHAPEL-ROOM,

N interesting apartment of ancient date, which, although much disguised, by white paint and bad modern flooring, has enough of originality left to gratify those who delight in the investigation of the arts and habits of by-gone days, and to revel in the pleasures produced by historical recollections. The ceiling is of oak panelled, and is slightly elevated in the centre ; the windows project, and are divided by mullions into quatrefoil-headed compartments, subdivided by transoms. The flat space between the two windows was formerly open, but has been closed by modern boarding. The walls of the room are hung with tapestry, representing the history of Noah : a picture of David meeting Abigail, over the fire-place, and a cabinet made of the wood of the sweet chesnut, and ornamented with ebony, with a few minor articles, complete the list of its furniture.

One subject there is, however, that it would be unpardonable to forget. Conspicuously placed upon the cabinet just mentioned is a group of figures, finely carved, relating to the crucifixion. It reminds us of the lonely-imprisoned queen Mary of Scots, by whom it was presented to the earl of Dorset. To her it was probably an object of religious homage and devotion, and we cannot but view it with respect and interest, from the long train of incidents which it recalls. The room receives from it an additional charm, and may be esteemed a shrine well calculated to contain so valuable a relic.

Two small rooms on the left of the entrance to the chapel require notice, from the decorations allusive to the family of the builder; one of these rooms contains the chimney-piece, with inscription and cognizances, represented in an engraving given in the first page of this volume; the other, a closet, has a small window diapered with knots and oak-leaves,

the latter said to have been borne by archbishop Bourchier to shew his maternal descent from the daughter of Thomas of Wood-
stock, duke of Gloucester.   In this closet
is a projection covered with brick, for which
we can find no other use than to place the
censer or incense-pots upon, and, till some
other be found, we may perhaps be indulged in believing this probable, for, after
having been used in the chapel, filled
with burning charcoal, it must have been
unsafe to have left them on wood; and if we
suppose the adjoining apartment to have
been the sacristry, or vestry, this will not appear very unlikely, as the fire-place before-
mentioned could have furnished the live
embers required.

These apartments are not shewn to visitors, but their ancient connexion with the
chapel would have rendered the description
of that edifice less complete, had they been
omitted.

## THE CHAPEL.

HIS ancient edifice, al-
though its furniture
and embellishments
have undergone great
alterations, still re-
tains its interesting
character. It has a
row of open seats on each side, with a pulpit
and desk opposite each other, a dwarf wain-
scotting being carried round the whole,
including the space railed and occupied by
the communion-table.

The family-pew or closet is raised, and
crosses the end of entrance; it is supported
in front by a screen of older date than the
superstructure, the head of the door-way,
with its spandrils, exhibiting remains of much
beauty; it has been cut lower to accommodate the new work, but enough is left in
the oak-leaf and the 𝕭𝖊𝖓𝖊𝖉𝖎𝖈𝖙𝖚𝖘 𝕯𝖊𝖚𝖘,
to ascertain its date and builder. The front
of the gallery or pew is ornamented by a

sort of screen or enriched frame-work of three openings (formerly filled with glass), surmounted by appropriate decorations, the family arms being emblazoned in the centre. The furniture and hangings of the closet, pulpit, communion-table and desk, are of crimson velvet and cloth of gold, brought from France by John, third duke of Dorset. Two pieces of stained glass in the side windows are considered curious; the remainder being small pieces in two colours, fragments of scripture, history, and legend, forming their subjects.

The ceiling, now a plaistered imitation of vaulting, was formerly panelled with oak, painted blue and starred with silver: pictures hung on the walls, and a tapestry of Christ before Pilate was suspended in the family seat above. The alterations were chiefly made by John, third duke, previous to whose time it was in a state of great neglect, and had not been used for many years. Divine service is now performed here by the family chaplain every Sunday afternoon; her ladyship attending the parish church of Sevenoaks in the morning.

Beneath the chapel is a fine crypt, with a vaulted roof supported by cross-springers arising from corbels. Its proportions are spoiled by a brick wall being built across the middle, to accommodate the conservatories with stowage for fuel. There have been openings in the walls, and there are now two entrances, besides indications of an apartment beyond.

The general access to the chapel is from the water-court, by a staircase and a handsome stone doorway (see engraving), the iron ring which forms a handle to the ancient oaken door being curiously ornamented with entwining lizards; but the visitor enters it from the chapel-room only; thus viewing the interior of the chapel from the family pew.

# THE BALL-ROOM,

A CHEERFUL and elegant apartment, has a noble marble chimney-piece, is surrounded by a frieze composed of figures of the strangest shapes, in most varied postures, and is otherwise decorated with a profusion of masks and quaint carvings, well drawn and boldly executed; which, together with its beautifully carved and gilt sconces, chairs with satin-wood backs, and numerous other elegant ornaments, cannot fail to attract attention.

The walls are decorated with family portraits, and some few others; namely—

*Robert, second Earl of Dorset.*—Deheers.
*Margaret, second Countess* .... Ditto.
Other Archer, sixth Earl of Plymouth.
—*Phillips.* Deemed an excellent likeness.

George John Frederic, fourth Duke.—
*Sanders.* A pleasing full-length portrait of the lamented young nobleman.

Arabella Diana, third Duchess.—*Hopner.*

*John Frederick, third Duke.*—Sir J. Reynolds. A magnificent Reynolds, both
in colouring and design.

Elizabeth, first Duchess.—*Hudson.*

*Lionel, first Duke.*—Sir G. Kneller.

Mary, fourth Countess.—*Mytens.*

*Edward, fourth Earl.*—Vandyke. A
noble full-length.

*Lord George Sackville* (49).—Gainsborough. A fine portrait, partaking, in a
high degree, of the truth, freedom,
vigour, and natural expression, generally found in the works of this painter.

Queen Charlotte.—*Romney,* after Reynolds.

King George III . . . . . . Ditto.

Ann, third Countess.—*Mytens.*

Richard, third Earl. . . . Ditto.

Frances, fifth Countess. Ditto.

Thomas, first Earl.—*C. Jansen.*

*Charles, sixth Earl.*—Sir G. Kneller.

Richard, fifth Earl.

Among the articles of vertu in this room are some busts, including one in marble of the third duchess, one of earl Whitworth, her second lord, and a plaister one of the emperor Alexander of Russia.

## THE CRIMSON DRAWING-ROOM.

THIS is the room of rooms for its pictures, nearly all of which are of first-rate excellence.

1. *A Sybil.*—Dominichino.  A countenance of great beauty and power, with eyes rapt in contemplation of kindred stars.
2. *Mary, Queen of Scots.*—Zucchero.
3. *A Magdalene.*—Guercino.
4. A Party going out of a morning.— *Wouvermans.*

*Cupids at Play.*—Parmegiano. A perfect gem, the design and execution equally meritorious, and the painting exquisitely delicate.

*Count Ugolino* (67).—Sir J. Reynolds. A striking contrast to the Fortune-teller, which hangs opposite, and an instance of the varied powers of this great English painter, of whose compositions this is generally considered the *chef d'œuvre.* It is a noble picture, though the subject is a painful one. The colouring is extremely rich and vigorous, and the light and shade finely managed. It was purchased by the Duke of Dorset for 400 guineas.

*Death of the Maccabees.*—Vandyke. A fine sketchy picture, with powerful effect of light and shade.

King Henry VIII.—*Holbein.*

*Cosmo, Duke of Tuscany.*—Tintoretto.

Madonna and Child.—After *Raphael.*

Wise Men's Offering.—*M. de Ferara.*

*Frances, fifth Countess of Dorset.*— Vandyke. A splendid portrait, of refined taste and finished execution. The drapery is most gracefully arranged, and admirably painted.

13. *Judith with the Head of Holofernes.*—Garafuli. A clever, highly-finished picture, by a painter whose works are seldom seen.

14. *Holy Family.*—Vandyke. Small.

15. *Flemish Wake.*—D. Teniers.

16. Marriage of St. Katharine.—*Parme-giano.*

17. St. John and Lamb.—*Schidoni.*

18. *Duchess of Cleveland* (68) —Sir P. Lely.

19. The Angel liberating St. Peter; or, the Guard-room.—*D. Teniers.* A carefully finished picture, of great merit.

20. Card-players.—*Ostade.*

21. A Dead Christ.—*L. Caracci.*

22. A Family of Beggars.—*Jan Mel.*

23. A Head, supposed of Raphael, by himself.

24. Flemish Musician.—*Teniers.*

25. Flemish Boy . . . . . . Ditto.

26. *Dejanira and Centaur.*—L. Caracci.

27. *Robinetta.*—Sir J. Reynolds. The original of the popular print; and cer-

tainly an exquisite picture, in conception, design, and colouring.

28. *The Fortune-teller.*—Sir J. Reynolds. Another deservedly popular picture, by the same master; the subject well-chosen, the colouring rich and harmonious, and the individual expression excellent. It was exhibited in 1777, and purchased[by the Duke of Dorset for 350 guineas.

29. *Holy Family.*—Titian.

30. The Nativity.—*Paul Veronese.*

31. Angel liberating St. Peter.—*Trevisani.*

32. Madonna, Infant, and St. Jerome.—*And. del Sarto.* A fine specimen of the master, elaborately finished and in excellent preservation.

33. *The Call of Samuel.*—Sir J. Reynolds. Appears to have been a favourite subject, from its having been repeatedly painted by him; has great breadth and freedom of handling, and the upturned countenance is very expressive.

34. *Landscape.*—Berghem. Not very highly finished, yet still a beautiful composi-

tion, with a pleasing warmth of colour, and a free delicate touch.

35. Holy Family.

36. *A Chinese Youth* (69).—Sir J. Reynolds.

The chimney-piece of this room is remarkable for its finely-sculptured marble. In the fire-place is a pair of very large silver dogs, and several nic-nacs are lying about the apartment, as some curious canes, a stiletto, &c. The high-backed chairs of the old school, now coming into vogue again, may also deserve notice.

## THE CARTOON GALLERY;

So named from its containing copies in oil, by Daniel Mytens, of six of the celebrated cartoons* of Raphael. These copies were painted for Lionel, Earl of

* The cartoons of Raphael, preserved in Hampton Court Palace, are *seven* in number : " Paul preaching at Athens," is the one not copied by Mytens. It may be acceptable, probably, to our younger readers, to know, that those car-

Middlesex, and removed to Knole from Copthall, in Essex, by Charles, Earl of Dorset.
They are as follow :

The Death of Ananias.

Elymas the Sorcerer.

Healing of the Lame Man.

The Miraculous Draught of Fishes.

Christ's Charge to Peter.

Paul and Barnabas at Lycaonia.

They are executed with great fidelity and
skill, and are in good preservation. The
gallery which they ornament is eighty-
nine feet and a half long, and contains,
besides the cartoons, the following pictures :

Charles, sixth Earl of Dorset.

Mary, sixth Countess.

*King George the Fourth* (in regimentals),
full-length.—Sir Thomas Lawrence.

toons (so called from being painted on *carta, cartona,* sheets
of paper) were executed by Raphael to the order of Pope
Leo X., as patterns for tapestry, to decorate the Papal
chapel at Rome. They were completed about the year
1520, and the tapestry was wrought at the famous manu-
factory of Arras, in Flanders. The cartoons themselves
were purchased for king Charles I., by Rubens, the painter.

X

*Robert Dudley, Earl of Leicester.**

Girl raising a Curtain.—*Mosnier.*

*The Earl of Surrey* (full-length).—Holbein.

*Portrait.†*—Dobson.

Chief-Baron Lant.

The sculptured marble chimney-piece of this room is also noticeable. Here, again, are a large pair of silver dogs, several silver sconces and chandeliers, and other articles, including a treasurer's chest of office, which belonged to the first earl of Dorset. In a recess in this apartment are four casts from the Florentine gallery—the Venus de Medicis, the Wrestlers, the Dancing Faun, and the Listening Slave. In the windows of this apartment are numerous armorial bearings, execu-

---

* Or, said by some to be " the marquess of Hertford, of Queen Elizabeth's time." It is, at all events, a most striking likeness of the earl of Leicester; add to which, that there was no such dignity as that of *marquess* of Hertford until the year 1640. It is a good painting.

† Said to be of General Monk, earl of Albemarle, or of lord Capel: certainly not at all resembling the likenesses of Monk. It is a clever portrait, in the style of Vandyke.

ted with great accuracy. Twelve of them appear to belong to families not in any way connected with the Sackvilles, nor traceable as possessors of Knole. They are as follow:—Richard Cole, of the Arches; Ralph Rokesby, master of Requests; Roger Manwode, chief-baron of Exchequer; Christopher Wray, lord-chief-justice; William Lewyn, judge of the Prerogative; Julius, judge of Admiralty; William Aubrey, judge of Audience; John Herbert, master of Requests; Snagge, master-serjeant at law; Gilbert Gerrard, master of Requests; John Popham, attorney-general; John Purkirage, serjeant-at-law. Many of these would seem to have been the law-officers of the crown at a time when the estate of Knole was in the hands of government. The other heraldic designs are the achievements of the Sackvilles and their wives, with one or two exceptions, in a direct line from Robert de Sackville to Richard the third Earl. In the windows of a colonnade in the house, these are made perfect to the time of the first duke, but this colonnade is not publicly shewn.

## THE KING'S BED-ROOM.

IN this room there is but one picture, namely, the Coligni Family,* by *Jansen;* containing portraits of the cardinal of that name and his two brothers.

The walls are lined with tapestry, in good preservation, on which is represented the story of Ne-buchadnezzar. The state bed, which cost £8,000, is also very perfect considering its age; this apartment, with its furni ture, having been prepared for the re ception of James I. The bedstead is pro-fusely ornamented, with a canopy-top; and the furniture (which begins to show symp-toms of not lasting for ever) is of gold and silver tissue, lined with rose-coloured satin, embroidered and fringed with gold and silver. About the room are several chairs

* See Appendix, No. 70.

and stools, covered to correspond with the furniture of the bed; also a handsome couch, carved and gilt, with purple-velvet cushions and pillow, embroidered with gold and silver, and a carved chair, cane-backed, with damask cushions. The tables are of chased silver. The expense of the entire fittings of the room are stated at £20,000. On the dressing-table, stands a complete toilet-service of silver, of excellent work manship, which was purchased by the first duke of Dorset, in 1743, at a sale of the effects of the countess of Northampton. In dependently of these ornaments, there is a profusion of silver in this apartment—mas sive urns, flower-pots, sconces, filligree baskets, censers, &c. Here are also two cabinets, one of ebony, and the other of ebony and ivory. The latter, the interior of which is very minute and curious, con tains two chamberlain's keys of office, and is decorated with relievos from scripture history.

## THE DINING-PARLOUR.

ERE it was that the parliamentary commissioners held their court of sequestration, in 1645, in the time of Edward, fourth earl of Dorset, whom they deprived, for a time, of this property. Here, too, we may suppose, that Charles, the sixth earl, in pleasanter days, assembled round his festive board Dryden, Prior, Pope, Wycherley, Congreve, Killigrew, Durfey, and others, eminent for wit or genius.

Its walls are devoted, almost exclusively, to portraits of poets, authors, and painters, of whom here is a brilliant assemblage :—

1. Waller.—*Jarvis.*
2. Addison.—Ditto.
3. *Sir T. Mayence,* Dutch physician to king James I.—Dobson.

4. Sir Walter Raleigh.
5. *Vandyke and Lord Gowrie.*—Vandyke.
6. *Locke.*—Sir G. Kneller.
7. *Hobbes.*—Ditto.
8. *Sir Isaac Newton.*—Ditto.
9. Flatman (a poet and painter, died 1688).
   —By himself.
10. Cowley.—*Du Boyce.*
11. Earl of Rochester.—Ditto.
12. Hugo Grotius.—*Tito Maio.*
13. Corelli (the composer).—Ditto.
14. Sir Charles Sedley.—*Kneller.*
15. Durfey.
16. Fletcher.
17. A Conversation-Piece; in which the
    painter has introduced himself, catching
    a likeness of Durfey the poet, while
    conversing with Mr. Buck, the family
    chaplain, and Mr. Lowin, the steward.
    The other figures are—George Allen, a
    clothier, of Sevenoaks, Mother Moss,
    and Jack Randall, the steward's-room
    boy.— *Vandergucht.*
18. Villiers, Duke of Buckingham.
19. *Dr. Johnson.*—Sir J. Reynolds.

20. *Sacchini* (the composer).—Ditto.

21. *Sir Joshua Reynolds.*—Ditto.

22. Sir Walter Scott.—*Phillips.*

23. *Garrick.*—Sir J. Reynolds.

24. *Goldsmith.*—Ditto.

25. *Burke.*—Opie.

26. Mrs. Catherine Phillips.

27. *Gay.*—Boll.

28. Handel.—*Denner.*

29. Ben Jonson.

30. Congreve.—After *Kneller.*

31. Wycherley.—Ditto.

32. Shakspeare.

33. Rowe.—After *Kneller.*

34. Garth.—Ditto.

35. Dryden.—*Kneller.*

36. Cartwright.

37. Swift.

38. *Otway.*—Sir P. Lely.

39. Pope.

40. Betterton, the celebrated actor, died 1712.—*Kneller.*

41. Charles, sixth Earl of Dorset.—Ditto.

42. Sir Philip Sidney.

43. Chaucer.

44. *Mrs. Abington* (actress).—Sir J. Reynolds.
45. Prior.
46. Thomas, first Earl of Dorset, half-length.
47. Milton when young, (ditto).
48. Butler, three-quarter small.
59. Carew, three-quarter, over door.
60. Foote. A clever copy.

Leaving this room, the visitor will again recognise the passage leading to the principal staircase, having been through all the apartments which are now exhibited to the public. Those used by the family contain many choice specimens of art, in painting and sculpture; but the visitor not being admitted here, no good purpose would be answered by giving a description of their contents.

The feelings with which many would quit such a mansion, would be those of regret that their memories are not sufficient to retain any adequate portion of the interest which has been excited: to such persons, it is hoped that this volume will prove a welcome assistant, by affording them an opportunity of reading at their leisure an account

Y

of the contents of those rooms through which they have been conducted ; while to those who have become possessed of it, and have perused its contents before visiting the mansion, it may be the means of directing their attention to some particular articles and circumstances, which might otherwise escape notice, amidst the multiplicity of objects which surround them.

# APPENDIX;

CONTAINING

## Brief Biographical Notices

OF MOST OF THE

# EMINENT OR REMARKABLE PERSONAGES

WHOSE PORTRAITS ARE PRESERVED AT

## KNOLE HOUSE.

# APPENDIX.

### 1.—*John Lord Somers*

Was the son of an attorney at Worcester, where he was born in 1650. In 1675, he was entered of Trinity College, Oxford, and took the degree of B.A. in 1681, having previously (in 1676) been called to the bar. At about this period, he published several legal-political tracts on the rights of Englishmen, which attracted considerable attention, and contributed to his success as a lawyer. His practice at the bar was soon extensive; notwithstanding which, he found leisure for several poetical attempts.

In 1688, Somers was one of the counsel for the bishops, on which occasion, though at first objected to on account of his comparative youth, he succeeded in establishing a character for profound constitutional learning.

After the Revolution, Mr. Somers was returned to parliament for Worcester, and acted a conspicuous part in the important debates of that period. About 1690, he was knighted and made solicitor-general; in 1692, attorney-general; in 1693, lord-keeper of the Great Seal; and in 1697, lord Chancellor, with the title of baron Somers. Of this office he was deprived in 1700, during a temporary ascendency of the Tory party; and in the following year he was impeached on some frivolous charges, but the impeachment not being supported, was of course acquitted. The king lived to express regret at having lost lord Somers from his council, but not long enough to form a new ministry, which was in contemplation when his majesty died.

After the accession of Queen Anne, lord Somers interfered but little in public life: his chief delight was literature. He was, however, President of the Council in 1708 & 9; but in 1710 again retired. He died in 1716, a bachelor.

Of his character, Horace Walpole says:—" All the traditional accounts of him, the historians of the last age, and its best authors, represent him as the most incorrupt lawyer, and the honestest statesman; as a master-orator, a genius of the finest taste, and a patriot of the noblest and most extensive views." And bishop Burnet says, " he was very learned in his own profession,

with a great deal more learning in other profes-
sions ; in divinity, philosophy, and history. He
had a great capacity for business, with an extra-
'ordinary temper ; so that he had all the patience
and softness, as well as the justice and equity,
becoming a great magistrate. ''

Lord Somers was an industrious collector of
tracts and manuscripts. Most of the latter were
destroyed by a fire in Lincoln's Inn in 1752.
The former were republished some years back
under the superintendence of Sir Walter Scott.

### 2.—*Don John of Austria,*

A natural son of the emperor Charles V, and a
distinguished military commander of the sixteenth
century, gained the famous battle of Lepanto, in
which upwards of 20,000 Turks perished, took
Tunis and Biserta, and afterwards, in the Netherlands, beat the allied armies at Gemblours, in
1578. He died the same year, aged 32.

### 3.—*The Duke of Parma.*

Alexander Farnese, duke of Parma and Placentia,
the son of Octavius Farnese, duke of Parma, and
Margaret, natural daughter of the emperor Charles
V., was present, at the age of eighteen, at the
battle of Lepanto, under Don John of Austria.
He was appointed, in 1578, governor of the

Netherlands, where his military achievements were most brilliant. He was wounded and died at Arras, in 1592, aged 46.

### 4.—*Henry of Lorraine, Duc de Guise,*

Surnamed Balafré (from a wound in the cheek), "one of the handsomest, wittiest, most courageous, and eloquent men of his time," but of ambitious and turbulent disposition, was the eldest son of Francis, duke of Guise, and born in 1550. As soon as he was able to bear arms, he served in Hungary and in France, and gave unquestionable proofs of his valour and capacity. He commanded the rear-guard at the battle of Jarnac, 1569, and at Chateau Thierry received the wound which caused him to be afterwards known by the designation of Balafré (gashed in the face). He married Catherine of Cleves, after which, he placed himself at the head of the army of the celebrated league projected by his uncle, the cardinal of Lorraine. His successes appear to have induced him to demand of Henry III. of France, unreasonable returns for his services : he was ordered to quit Paris, but soon re-entered in triumph, and compelled the king to fly from his capital. Henry now resorted to the base resolution of causing his assassination : under pretence of adjusting their differences, he appointed to meet the duke at Blois, where he was murdered on entering the room in which the king held his court, Dec. 23, 1588, aged 38.

### 5.—*Charles Duc de Bourbon, Constable of France, born 1489,*

Was the third of his name, and as eminent for his military talents as for his errors and misfortunes. The hatred of the mother of Francis I, and a long succession of indignities, induced him to swerve from his loyalty to his king and relative. He corresponded with the emperor Charles V, the enemy of France, whom he engaged to assist in an invasion of the kingdom. The king was apprised of this treason by two of the constable's attendants, but disbelieving the possibility of such baseness, refused to arrest him. He crossed the Rhone into Italy, and was in the action in which the Imperials attacked the French troops in the Milanese, and subsequently in that in which the French king was defeated at Pavia. Bourbon had, in 1526, the command of the Imperial army, and marching against the Papal territories, he led his troops to the gates of Rome, which he assaulted on three different sides. The assailants were at first repulsed; and Bourbon, in the act of rallying them, received a musket-ball, as he was mounting a scaling-ladder in the trenches. His death, he felt, was certain; but he ordered

z

his body to be covered with a cloak, to conceal the disaster from his army, and thus died, in May 1527, aged 38.

## 6.—*Ann de Montmorenci, Peer, Marshal, and Constable of France, born 1493,*

Was one of the greatest generals of the 15th century. In 1512, he successfully defended the city of Menziers against the emperor Charles V; and in 1525, he was taken prisoner with king Francis I. at the battle of Pavia, which was fought contrary to his advice. He was made constable of France, in 1538, and afterwards experienced various revolutions of fortune, both at court and in the field. He died of a wound received at the battle of St. Denis, on the 12th Nov. 1567, aged 74. Being covered with blood and wounds, a cordelier offered to prepare him for death, but he replied in a firm voice, " Do you think that a man who has lived nearly eighty years with honour, has not learned to die for a quarter of an hour ?"

## 7. — *Henry Howard, Earl of Northampton,*

Was brother to Thomas, duke of Norfolk, and son of the earl of Surrey, beheaded by Henry

VIII. He was made earl of Northampton and lord-treasurer by king James I. It is believed of this nobleman that he was privy to the murder of Sir Thomas Overbury; independently of which his character will bear but little scrutiny. He favoured the entrance of the jesuits into this kingdom, and avowed, in a letter under his own hand, that he was a Protestant only in show, while his heart was with the Catholics. He died in 1613, constable of Dover Castle, and Warden of the Cinque Ports, Lord Privy Seal, and chancellor of the university of Cambridge. His malignancy may be inferred from his declaring that " he would be content to be damned perpetually in hell, to be revenged of that proud Welchman, Sir Richard Mansel." He built Northumberland House, in the Strand, first called Northampton House, and afterwards Suffolk House.

### 8.—*Francis, Duc de Guise.*

The father of Henry, duc de Guise (of whom see No. 4.) Of the life of the elder duke, nothing that is remarkable is related.

### 9.—*Herbert, Earl of Pembroke,*

. Was born in the reign of Henry VIII, the son of a Welch knight, and bred to arms. In the 5th

Edward VI, he first distinguished himself by quelling an insurrection in Wiltshire. In 1551, he was created earl of Pembroke, and he became one of the most powerful noblemen of his time, taking an active part in public affairs, both as a statesman and a soldier. In 1553, he performed the signal service to queen Mary, of surrounding and taking prisoners, Sir Thos. Wyatt and four thousand of his followers. It is recorded of this nobleman that, at about this period, he rode to his mansion of Baynard Castle, " with three hundred horsemen in his retinue, of whom one hundred were gentlemen in plain blue cloth, with chains of gold, and badges of a dragon on their sleeves."—He died on the 17th March, 1569-70 (11th of Elizabeth), and was buried in St. Paul's on the 8th April following, with such magnificence, that the mourning given at his funeral cost the very large sum, at that period, of £2,000.*

### 10.—*John Dudley, duke of Northumberland,*

Was the son of Edmund Dudley, executed in 1510. He was restored to his inheritance about 1514, by Henry VIII, who created him lord

* Stowe.

Dudley and viscount Lisle, and honoured him with command as well by sea as by land. He distinguished himself by his valour and prudence, and was in consequence elevated to the title of earl of Warwick. For further particulars concerning the life and ignominious death of this nobleman, who was one of the possessors of Knole, see p. 10.

## 11.—*Roger Bacon, commonly called Friar Bacon, b.* 1214.

A Franciscan friar, of extraordinary genius and learning, was born near Ilchester, in Somersetshire. He studied first at Oxford, and afterwards at Paris, and made rapid progress in scientific attainments. About 1240, he returned to Oxford, and, assuming the Franciscan habit, prosecuted experimental philosophy with unremitting ardour; pure mathematics, astronomy, medicine, chemistry, and judicial astrology, were discussed by him with extraordinary ability. This astonishing progress in sciences which, in that ignorant age, were totally unknown to the rest of mankind, instigated the malice and envy of his brother monks, who, propagating the report (and perhaps thinking so) that such knowledge must be the result of supernatural aid, accused him of dealing with the devil. His lectures were stopped; his writings prohibited; and he himself, in 1278,

imprisoned in his cell.    Here, being allowed
books, he continued his studies, corrected his
former labours, and wrote several curious pieces.
At the expiration of ten years, being then
seventy-four years old, he was released by order
of pope Jerome, and he died in 1294, aged 80.
Such are the few particulars which are known of
this wonderful man, who shone in his age like a
single bright star in a dark hemisphere.

## 12.—*John Wickliffe, the Reformer,*

Was born in 1324, in the bishopric of Durham,
and educated at Merton College, Oxford; of
which, by the seculars of the society, he was
chosen principal.    This choice was opposed by
the monks, who, appealing to the papal authority,
caused Wickliffe and his party to quit the college.    He retired to a living which he had at
Lutterworth, in Leicestershire, and here commenced an enquiry concerning the pope's authority in temporal matters, and urged his arguments
both in writing and preaching.    His doctrines
were in some degree countenanced at the time
both by king and nobles, and they may be considered as prefatory to those of Luther, one hundred and fifty years afterwards, which achieved
the Reformation.    Finding that his doctrines
were gaining ground, Simon Sudbury, archbishop

of Canterbury, assembled a council at Lambeth, and cited Wickliffe to appear. He obeyed,* being accompanied by the duke of Lancaster, to whose presence, and the known support of other noblemen, he is supposed to have owed his acquittal. The pope urged further proceedings; but the English churchmen, knowing the influence by which Wickliffe was likely to be supported, contented themselves with enjoining his future silence. He died at Lutterworth in 1384.

### 13.—*Stephen Gardiner, Bishop of Winchester, and Chancellor of England,*

Was born at Bury St. Edmund's, in 1483. He was natural son to Richard Woodville,† a brother of Elizabeth, queen of Edward IV. His mother married a servant named Gardiner, from whom he took his name. He was educated at Cambridge, and afterwards became secretary to cardinal Wolsey. In this capacity, he drew up the treaty of alliance with Francis I, and having attracted the notice of Henry VIII, he was sub-

---

* This scene is represented in a fine painting, called the " Citation of Wickliffe," from which a beautiful print has been taken.

† According to some authorities, to Dr. Lionel Woodville, bishop of Salisbury, brother of Richard.

sequently sent to Rome to negociate the king's divorce from Katharine of Arragon. On his return, he was made archdeacon of Norfolk, and soon afterwards secretary of state. He obtained the consent of the university of Cambridge to the king's divorce, and, as a recompense, was raised to the rich see of Winchester. He introduced Cranmer to Henry VIII. In 1533, he went ambassador to France; and on his return he wrote his treatise " De Verâ et Falsâ Obedientiâ," in favour of the king's supremacy, a doctrine which he himself afterwards refused to conform to, for which he was imprisoned during the greater part of the reign of Edward VI. By queen Mary he was at once released, and made chancellor; after which, until his death, he became the sanguinary tool of that queen's bigotry and vengeance. He died at Whitehall, in 1555, aged 72, expressing great remorse on his death-bed, and exclaiming frequently, " Erravi cum Petro, sed non flevi cum Petro"— I have sinned with Peter, but I have not wept with Peter.

## 14.—*Sir James Wilford*

Was knighted by the Protector Somerset, in 1547. He was distinguished as a military commander, for his gallant defence of Haddington, New

Brunswick, against the French and Scots ; but little more is known of him.

## 15.—*George Clifford, Earl of Cumberland,*

Was descended from the ancient family of that name, and born at Brougham Castle, in Westmoreland, in 1558. He was educated at Cambridge ; after leaving which, he fitted out a small fleet, for discovery or plunder, and distinguished himself in annoying the Spanish armada, and afterwards in plundering their settlements. He was a noted cavalier at tilts and tournaments, on which occasions he wore on his high-crowned hat a glove, ornamented with diamonds, given to him by queen Elizabeth ; he was also a desperate horse-racer. When the gallant Sir Henry Lee resigned the office of champion, her majesty conferred the honour on the earl of Cumberland ;* the armour he wore is said to be now preserved in Appleby Castle. He lived with Margaret, his countess, with cold reserve, and died in the Savoy in 1605, leaving one daughter, Anne, afterwards married to Richard, earl of Dorset.

* For many entertaining particulars, see " Walpole's Memoirs."

## 16.—*John Fisher, Bishop of Rochester.*

This learned and pious prelate, and virtuous man, was born at Beverley, in Yorkshire, in 1459. His father, a merchant, died at an early age, and the mother sent her son, first to Beverley school, and thence to Cambridge, where he became fellow of Trinity College, and in 1495, proctor of the university. He was elected to be confessor to Margaret, countess of Richmond, mother of king Henry VII, and was subsequently made bishop of Rochester, in which dignity he died, having constantly refused to change it for wealthier preferment—" he would never" he said, " quit his old wife, for one that was richer." He distinguished himself, from conscientious motives, as an opponent of Luther, disputed the king's supremacy, and sided with the queen on the divorce question. He denied the king's supremacy in convocation, in 1531, and refusing to take the oath of allegiance to the king and his heirs by Ann Boleyn, he was committed to the Tower, subsequently tried and found guilty of high treason, and was beheaded, 22nd June, 1535.

## 17.—*Thomas Cranmer, Archbishop of Canterbury,*

Was the son of Thomas Cranmer, Esq. of Aslacton, Notts, where he was born in 1489. At the age of fourteen, he was admitted of Jesus College, Cambridge, of which he afterwards became a fellow; but vacated his fellowship and quitted the college, on his marriage. After the death of his wife, he was re-admitted. He took the degree of D.D., and was made the logical lecturer and examiner. While the plague raged at Cambridge, he retired to a relative's at Waltham Abbey, and here he met Fox, the king's almoner, and Gardiner, secretary to Wolsey. Discussing the question of the validity of the king's marriage with Katharine, he expressed his opinion that the point at issue was simply this, " whether or not a man may marry his brother's wife." This was reported to the king, who exclaimed, " this fellow has got the right sow by the ear," sent for Cranmer to court, and made him one of his chaplains. He composed a vindication of the intended divorce, and was sent to France, Italy, and Germany, to promote the king's views. During this journey, he married a second wife. In 1533, he returned to England, and was consecrated archbishop of Canterbury. In the

ensuing year, he pronounced the sentence of divorce between Henry and Katharine, and married
the king to Ann Boleyn.

Being at the head of the church, he now ex-
erted himself in the business of the Reformation;
the Bible was translated into English and monasteries dissolved, chiefly by his means. In
1536, he divorced the king from Ann Boleyn.
He afterwards endeavoured to abolish the super-
stitious observance of holidays, and he spoke
three days in the House of Lords against the sanguinary Act of the Six Articles; and though it
then passed, he, in 1542, succeeded in moderating
its rigour by an act of his own. After Lord
Cromwell's death, he retired into privacy; but
the king continued his protection to him, and at
his death appointed him one of the executors to
his will, and one of the regents of the kingdom.

In 1546, he crowned Edward VI., during
whose short reign he promoted the Reformation
to the utmost of his power, and was particularly
instrumental in establishing the Liturgy and the
thirty-nine articles. He first opposed lady Jane
Grey, but at length, from importunity, favoured
her pretensions. For this, and his well-known
religious principles, he was, on queen Mary's
accession, committed to the Tower, and in the
ensuing parliament attainted and found guilty of
high-treason. In April, 1554, he was removed

to Oxford, with Ridley and Latimer, who had
been also convicted, and here, after the most ag-
gravated insult, he was thrown into a dungeon,
where, from promises held out to him, he was
flattered and frightened into a written recantation
of the Protestant faith. This was circulated
throughout the kingdom, in order to degrade him;
but the vengeance of the Romanists did not stop
here: on the 24th February, 1556, a writ was
signed for his being burned at the stake, and on
the 24th March he was so executed, near Baliol
college, Oxford. Dr. Cole preached a funeral
sermon over him in St. Mary's church, the unhappy Cranmer being placed on a kind of stage
next the pulpit. At the end of the sermon, he
was desired to make a public profession of his
faith, which he did in the most emphatic manner,
renouncing the Pope as Antichrist, and proclaim-
ing himself a true Protestant, and denying the
truth of the paper written by his hand contrary
to the thoughts of his heart. After this he was
hurried to execution, and, being fastened to the
stake, he first thrust into the flames the hand
which had signed the recantation, crying out frequently " this hand hath offended, this unworthy
right hand," and died calmly and resolutely, with
his eyes raised towards heaven, and exclaiming,
" Lord Jesu, receive my spirit!"

His character has been equally the subject of exaggerated praise and of undeserved censure. The worst feature in it is, that he was himself intolerant in religious matters; for, as to the charge against him of concurring too readily in the unjustifiable measures of Henry VIII. against his wives, it should not be forgotten that, considering the circumstance to which he owed his first footing at court, but little independence could be expected from him on such a subject. Of his death, Dr. Southey says, " of all the martyrdoms during this great persecution, this was, in all its circumstances, the most injurious to the Romish cause."

### 18.—*Thomas Cromwell, Earl of Essex,*

Is said to have been the son of a blacksmith at Putney, where he was born in 1480. He was a man of no learning, but of strong natural abilities, improved by travelling and observation. He was patronized by Cardinal Wolsey, by whom he was introduced to Henry VIII., who thought so favourably of him as to raise him to the earldom of Essex, and to appoint him lord-chamberlain and vicar-general. He employed his power in promoting the Reformation : he was the chief instrument of the suppression of monasteries, and the destruction of images and relics. He fell a victim to his zeal for the Protestant cause, and was sacrificed to the Roman Catholic party when the king had in view his marriage with Katharine Howard. He was beheaded July 30, 1540.

## 19.—*Sir Thomas More, Lord Chancellor,*

Was born in Milk-street, London, in 1480, the son of Sir John More, justice of the King's Bench. He became page to cardinal Moreton, archbishop of Canterbury and lord chancellor, who, predicting that " he would one day prove a miracle of men," sent him to Oxford, and afterwards to the inns of court. He soon after married the daughter of Mr. Colt, of New Hall, in Essex, and was elected into parliament. About 1505, he was made a justice of the King's Bench, and in 1508, judge of the Sheriff's court; at which period he found leisure to write his Utopia, and to correspond with the celebrated Erasmus. About 1516, he was made a master of Requests, and soon after knighted, and honoured with a seat at the Privy-council. In 1520, he was made treasurer of the Exchequer, and the king (Hen. VIII.) at this period was so familiar with him, that he called once at his house in Chelsea (it was in Beaufort-row, and pulled down in 1740) and partook of the family-dinner. In 1523, he was made speaker of the House of Commons.   After Wolsey's downfal, More was made lord-chancellor, he being the first layman ever raised to that dignity. He filled this office with integrity and diligence for three years, and resigned it in 1533, having previously declined his sanction to the king's divorce from Katharine.   He afterwards refused to take the oath of supremacy, for which he was arraigned, and executed on Tower Hill, July 5, 1535.   He was twice married, and left a son and four daughters by his first wife.

### 20.—*Thomas Howard, Duke of Norfolk,*

The eldest son of the earl of Surrey, beheaded by Henry VIII.  Queen Mary restored the son to his family honours, and allowed him to succeed to the title of his grandfather, the duke of Norfolk. By queen Elizabeth, he was made a knight of the garter, and otherwise favoured; until it was discovered that he aspired to a marriage with Mary queen of Scots, thereby to attain to the succession of the English throne, and that he had actually entered into a contract of marriage with her (after having been once released from arrest on his promise to relinquish such a design), and taken other measures, full particulars of which were communicated to the government.  Norfolk was committed to the Tower, tried in 1572, convicted on the clearest testimony, and beheaded. His fate was deeply deplored, and it is believed he would have been pardoned; but the proceedings of Mary's partisans were at this juncture so violent, that his execution was considered necessary by both houses of parliament.

## 21.—*Henry Fitz-Alan, Earl of Arundel,*

Was the son of Thomas, earl of Arundel, and born about the beginning of the sixteenth century. Of his early life few particulars are known. He was imprisoned as one of the conspirators against Dudley, duke of Northumberland, but released. He afterwards appeared to acquiesce in Northumberland's views in favour of Lady Jane Grey; but was no sooner in safety from the duke's machinations, than (from religious principle, it may be presumed, as he was of an old Catholic family) he declared for Mary, and was a chief promoter of her accession. He was constituted steward of the household during her reign, and in favour during that of her successor, in flattering whom, under the delusion that a marriage with himself was possible, he ruined his estate. He died in 1580; his daughter having previously married Thomas Howard, Duke of Norfolk, whence the earldom of Arundel in that family.

2 B

## 22.—*Cardinal Wolsey,*

Is said to have been the son of a butcher at Ipswich, where he was born in March 1471. He was educated, however, at Oxford, where he took a bachelor's degree at the age of fourteen, and soon after became a fellow of Magdalen college, and undertook the education of the three sons of Thomas Grey, marquess of Dorset, who, in 1500, presented him the living of Lymington, Somersetshire. After the marquess's death, by the influence of Denne, archbishop of Canterbury, he was made one of the chaplains to the king (Henry VII.), and rector of Redgrave, Norfolk, and was afterwards appointed to negociate the king's marriage with Margaret of Savoy; which affair he executed with such ability and dispatch that he was, in 1508, made dean of Lincoln.

On the accession of Henry VIII., he ingratiated himself so successfully with the young monarch, as almost to monopolize his favour for above sixteen years; during which he was raised, step by step, to the highest honours, ecclesiastical and civil; being, in 1515, lord chancellor of England, a Cardinal of Rome, the pope's legate, and holding all sorts of bishoprics and pensions, foreign as well as British, which made his income nearly equal to the king's. His retinue was inordinately splendid, his household consisting of nearly a thousand persons, among whom were many noblemen of the highest quality, who thought it no degradation to tend him at mass, serving the wine to him on their knees. The king had given himself up wholly to his direction, and Wolsey, in fact, reigned paramount. Intoxicated with power, he was vain, haughty, and imperious, suffering none but his own creatures to have any influence at court; he raised money by violent extortions, termed by him " loans," and " benevolences," dispensed with parliaments for fourteen years, and in their stead established a sort of inquisition, in which all power, civil and ecclesiastical, was virtually centred in himself; and at length nearly caused a revolution in the kingdom by his unbounded insolence and rapacity. This state of things could not last long : every fresh act of oppression served but to add to the certainty of his fall. The immediate cause of his overthrow was connected with the king's divorce ; but the dawning change in the religion of the country, and the general disgust felt against this tyrannic churchman by the nobility and gentry of England, completed his ruin. In the case of the divorce, Wolsey vacillated between his anxiety to serve the king and his fear of offending the pope. He thus displeased both ; while Ann Boleyn imputed her disappointment to him, and Queen Katharine and her party were indignant at the part he had already taken. He was thus left without a friend; his enemies gained the king's ear ; and the result was a message to resign the great seals. He was next ordered to quit York palace, which was seized by the king, together with all his furniture and plate, and he was directed to await the royal pleasure at his seat at Esher. After remaining here some time, he removed to Richmond ; but his enemies, still fearing his influence with the king, obtained an order for him to remain at his see (York). He had not been long there before he was arrested by the earl of Northumberland on a charge of high-treason. On his road to London, he fell sick at Sheffield, the seat of the earl of Shrewsbury, but pursued his journey as far as Leicester, where he died Nov. 30, 1530. Of his character, nothing can be said in praise, except that, during his administration no person was prosecuted for heresy, that he was impartial in his office of chancellor, and that from one of his worst faults, insatiable vanity, resulted an advantage to posterity in the several magnificent buildings erected by him—as Christ-church, Oxford, a college at Ipswich, and Hamptoncourt palace.

## 23.—*John Whitgift, Archbishop of Canterbury,*

Was of an ancient Yorkshire family, but born at Great Grimsby, in Lincolnshire, in 1530. From early youth he was prepossessed in favour of the reformed religion, and was expelled from the house of his aunt, a catholic, for refusing to go to mass. In 1548, he went to Queen's college, Cambridge; and thence to Pembroke-hall; and in 1555 he was chosen fellow of Peter-house; soon after which he entered into holy orders, and became so distinguished for learning and piety, that he was appointed one of the queen's chaplains. In 1572, he first entered into the celebrated controversy with the puritans, which was the means of advancing him to the deanery of Lincoln, the bishopric of Worcester, and, finally, in 1583, to the archbishopric of Canterbury. He died in 1604, leaving behind him the character of " a mild and peaceable man, who would have been glad to reclaim the puritans by gentle methods, according to the precepts of the gospel."* He was buried at Croydon, where he founded an hospital, and in the church of which town is a monument to his memory.

* Rapin.

### 24.—*Sir Francis Walsingham,*

Was born in 1536, and educated at King's college, Cambridge; after leaving which, he went the tour of Europe, and acquired a vast fund of information, most valuable to him in after-life. On the accession of Queen Elizabeth, he came to England, and was soon appointed ambassador to France; and on Sir William Cecil's promotion, he took his place as secretary of state, in which situation he displayed great sagacity in unravelling domestic conspiracies, and anticipating the designs of the several states of Europe. On every occasion in which political skill and penetration were necessary, Walsingham was sure to be employed; and he invariably acquitted himself to satisfaction. He died in 1590, so poor that his assets were scarcely sufficient to pay his funeral expenses. He was an active promoter of the navigation and commerce of the country, not only as a minister, but as a private speculator; probably to an extent beyond his means.

### 25.—*Thomas Egerton, Baron of Ellesmere,*

Was the natural son of Sir Richard Egerton, of Ridley, Cheshire, and born about 1540. He was

educated at Brazen-nose college, Oxford, and
went thence to Lincoln's-inn, where he soon
became eminent as a lawyer. In 1591, he was
made solicitor-general; the next year attorney-
general, and knighted; soon after, master of the
rolls, and then lord-keeper. In 1603, he was
made Baron Ellesmere, and lord chancellor; and
soon after, Viscount Brackley, and chancellor of
Oxford. He resigned in the early part of the
reign of James I.; and, died in 1616, with the
character of a learned, prudent, judicious, and
honest man.

### 26.—*William Cecil, Baron Burleigh,*

Was the son of Richard Cecil, esq., master of the
robes to Henry VIII., and born at Bourn, in Lincolnshire, in 1520. He received the rudiments of
education at Grantham, and about 1535 was entered of St. John's college, Cambridge, and became noted for classical learning. In 1545, he
entered himself of Gray's-inn; but the king,
hearing of his acquirements, gave him the reversion of the *custos brevium* (keeper of the writs),
worth £210 a year. About this time he married
the sister of Sir John Cheke, tutor to Edward VI.
In 1547, he was appointed master of requests, by
the Protector Somerset, whom he afterwards at-

tended on his expedition against the Scots. In
1548, Mr. Cecil was made secretary of state ; but in
the following year, Northumberland's faction pre-
vailing, he participated in the disgrace of the Protector, and was sent prisoner to the Tower. After
about three months' confinement, he was released ;
and in 1551, restored to his office, knighted, and
sworn of the privy council. In 1553, he was
made chancellor of the order of the garter.

On the death of Edward VI., Cecil had so far
evaded all direct participation in Northumberland's
attempt in favour of lady Jane Grey, that he was
received graciously at the court of queen Mary ;
but not choosing to change his religion, he relin-
quished his appointments. Queen Elizabeth's
accession dispelled the cloud which had obscured
his fortunes. He was at once made a privy-councillor, and reinstated in his office of secretary of
state. His first advice to the queen was, to call a
parliament ; and the first business that he proposed
was the establishment of a national church. A
plan of reformation was accordingly drawn up under
his auspices, and the legal establishment of the
church of England was the result. He next directed his attention to the regulation of the coinage,
which in preceding reigns had been greatly de-
based. In 1561, he was appointed master of the
wards ; and in 1571, created baron Burleigh, as

a reward for his services, especially in having suppressed the formidable northern rebellion. In 1572, he was honoured with the garter, and soon after, on the death of the marquess of Winchester, raised to the office of lord-high-treasurer, which he held till his death.

From this period we find Burleigh the prime mover of every material transaction during the reign of Elizabeth. Other favourites might have temporary influence, but in *him* she confided in all matters of importance. Having filled the highest offices for forty years, and guided the helm of government during the most glorious period of English history, he died, August 4, 1598, with perfect serenity, in the bosom of his family, aged seventy-eight.

He was a man equally remarkable for abilities and prudence; in his private character most amiable; in temper, cheerful; in disposition, generous and hospitable; and he was certainly one of the most able, upright, and indefatigable ministers, that the English annals can boast of. He left a large fortune to his posterity.

## 27.—*Sir Christopher Hatton,*

Was of a Lincolnshire family. He was entered of St. Mary-hall, Oxford, and afterwards studied the law at the Inner Temple, until made one of queen

Elizabeth's gentlemen-pensioners. His elegant
figure and manners (and graceful dancing, as is
said) recommended him to her majesty's notice,
and he rose progressively until he attained the
great seal, in 1587, when he was also honoured
with the garter. He held the office of chancellor
for four years, until his death, in 1591, but with
little credit for legal profundity. He possessed
some literary acquirements, and was a moderate,
prudent, and sensible man.

### 28.—*Robert Dudley, Earl of Leicester,*

One of the chief favourites of queen Elizabeth :
he was the son of John Dudley, Duke of Northumberland, and born in 1532. He of course
shared in the disgrace of his family during the
reign of Mary ; but, on the accession of Elizabeth, he was again noticed at court, and in a
short time was made master of the horse, a knight
of the garter, and privy-councillor, and was proposed as a suitable husband for the queen of
Scots. The death of Dudley's lady at this juncture, gave rise to very dark suspicions. In
1564, he was created baron Denbigh and earl of
Leicester, and made chancellor of Oxford. About
this period he married the dowager lady Sheffield,
but finding her in some degree a bar to his preferment at court, he is accused of an attempt to

poison her. His conduct towards both his wives was discussed at the time with great bitterness, in a pamphlet entitled, "A Dialogue between a Scholar, a Gentleman, and a Lawyer," which excited so much attention, that the queen herself caused letters to be written from the privy-council, vindicating Leicester's character.

In 1575, the queen visited her favourite at Kenilworth, where she was entertained for seventeen days, at an expense of £60,000. In 1585, he was sent as generalissimo to the Low Countries, where his conduct excited so much disgust that he was recalled ; yet he remained in favour with the queen, whom he is reported to have advised to get rid of the queen of Scots by poison.

His last office was that of lieutenant-general of the army at Tilbury. He died in 1588, when, if one half of the reports against him be true, the world was freed of a most accomplished villain. He is described as of handsome person (his face, *we* should think, excepted), a good speaker and writer, and possessing considerable literary acquirements. By the spirit of his conversation, the warmth of his flattery, and the expense of his entertainments, he maintained an ascendancy over the queen for the long period of thirty years. As a statesman, or a commander, he displayed but little ability. He sanctioned the Reformation, and was a strict observer of religious forms ; but

the whole course of his life contradicts the notion
of his real piety: his rapacity and ambition were
unbounded.

### 29.—*Charles Howard, Earl of Nottingham,*

An able statesman, and successful naval commander, in the reign of Elizabeth, was the son of
William Howard, baron Effingham, and born in
1536. He acquired his experience as a seaman
under his father, who was lord-high-admiral of
England till the accession of Elizabeth. He succeeded his father in title and estates in 1573; after
which he became lord-chamberlain; and in 1585,
was appointed lord-high-admiral, to act against
the Spanish armada. On this occasion he distinguished himself so conspicuously by repeated
attacks of a superior enemy, that a pension was
granted to him for life. In 1596, he commanded
the naval forces sent against Spain, and on his
return was created earl of Nottingham. He died
in 1624, aged eighty-seven.

### 30.—*Robert Cecil, Earl of Salisbury,*

The second son of Elizabeth's favourite minister,
the great Burleigh, and born about the year
1550. He was deformed, and of feeble constitution, on which account his early education was

confined to the house of his father. He was afterwards entered of St. John's-college, Cambridge, where he became a fellow, and took his degree. His first entrance into public was in the parliament of 1585-6, when he represented the city of Westminster, being then in his thirty-fifth year: for several subsequent years he was returned for the county of Herts. About 1590, he accompanied the earl of Derby to France, as secretary to the embassy; and on his return, in 1591, was knighted by queen Elizabeth, and made undersecretary of state to Sir Francis Walsingham; at whose death, in 1596, he succeeded as secretary of state.

As prime minister, Sir Robert Cecil appears to have successfully imitated the politics of his father. While Elizabeth lived, he maintained himself in her good opinion; and on her death he contrived to establish himself equally well with her successor, with whom he had even ventured to carry on a secret correspondence during the latter years of Elizabeth's life. One of the great objects of his policy appears to have been to secure the throne to James; accordingly we find him one of the first to proclaim that monarch, whom he met at York, and was immediately confirmed in all his offices by the new king, who spent four days at Cecil's princely seat of Theobald's before entering the capital.

In king James's first creation of peers, 20th
May, 1603, Cecil was raised to the barony of
Essenden; in August, 1604, he was made viscount Cranbourne; and in less than a year there-
after, earl of Salisbury, knight of the garter, and
chancellor of the university of Cambridge.   The
truth is, he suited himself so exactly to the temper
of his sovereign, that he became indispensable to
him, and was valued and rewarded accordingly.
He is accused of having leaned too much to the
royal prerogative, and of a servile compliance
with the king's wishes; yet he was ever most
zealous and active in the discharge of public
business; and in opposing the Spanish connexion,
he proved, for once at least, that his condescen-
sion for the king would not lead him all lengths.

The death of Sackville, earl of Dorset, made
way for Salisbury's preferment to his father's
office of lord-treasurer, which he held without
resigning that of secretary of state.   For about
four years he struggled with the embarrassed
finances of the crown; at one time opposing a just
and laudable economy to the wild profusion of the
king; at another (by unjustifiably raising the
custom-duties), pandering to his master's extravagance, involving himself in censure, and weak-
ening the stability of the Stuart dynasty.   It is
well, probably, for Salisbury's historical character, that he did not long survive.   He died at

Marlborough in 1612, after a tedious and painful
illness, aged fifty-one.   The general sentiment of
the nation towards his memory was unfavourable.
His hostility to Essex and Raleigh—his arbitrary
augmentation of the customs—his revival of feudal
exactions—his servility to the king's notions of
prerogative—and, above all, his assertion that
torture might lawfully be inflicted on Englishmen,
at their sovereign's pleasure,—were remembered
with bitterness against him.

He married Elizabeth, sister to Brooke, lord
Cobham, by whom he had a son and daughter.
His descendant James, the seventh earl, was ad-
vanced, in 1789, to the dignity of marquess.

## 31.—*Sir Francis Drake.*

This celebrated circumnavigator was the eldest of
the twelve sons of Edmund Drake, a mariner, and
born near Tavistock, Devon, in 1545.   He was
early apprenticed to the master of a small trading
vessel, who, dying unmarried, left him the ship
as a legacy.   Drake sold it, and embarked the
proceeds in an adventure to the then newly-dis-
covered West India islands.   He sailed from
England in the squadron of Captain John Hawkins, afterwards the celebrated Admiral, who
made him a purser, and soon after captain of a
ship to the gulf of Mexico, where, in consequence

of a treacherous attack by the Spanish fleet, four
out of six of the English vessels were destroyed.
Those of Hawkins and Drake were the two that
escaped.

By this adventure, Drake lost his whole property; but he soon projected a new expedition,
and having first made a voyage to inform himself
of the strength of the places he proposed visiting,
he returned, and, in May 1572, sailed with his
brother, John Drake, on a reprisal cruise against
the Spanish West India settlements. He set sail
in command of the Pasha, of 70 tons, and his
brother in the Swan, of 25 tons; the two supplied
with a year's provisions, and seventy-three men
and boys. With this inconsiderable force, aided
by one Captain Rause with a crew of about fifty
men, an attack was made on the town of Nombre
de Dios, but did not succeed. Shortly after, however, our adventurers had the good fortune to
capture a string of treasure-mules, on their
route from Panama, and they returned to Plymouth with considerable booty.

After this, we find Drake in the channel, assist-
ing the earl of Essex in suppressing the Irish rebellion. His services on this occasion induced
Essex and Sir Christopher Hatton to present him
to queen Elizabeth, who gave him the command
of five small vessels, and secretly countenanced
a voyage planned by him against the Spaniards in

the South Seas, which Drake proposed to reach through the straits of Magellan. The squadron was ostensibly fitted out for a trading voyage to Alexandria. On first sailing, they were driven back by a severe gale; but on the 13th Dec. 1577, they again put to sea, and on the 20th May 1578, the squadron anchored in Port St. Julian, off Magellan, in 40° 30′ south latitude. In September following, the squadron emerged from the western end of the straits, and Drake had soon the satisfaction of sailing an English ship on the South sea. On clearing the Straits, the fleet held a north-west course, but was driven by a gale into 57° south latitude, soon after which the Marigold was lost, and never afterwards heard of. The Golden Hind, in which Drake sailed, broke from her anchor and drove to sea. The Elizabeth, commanded by captain Winter, returned through the Straits, and reached England in safety: but Drake himself, beating round without the Strait, touched at Cape Horn, and thence along the coast to Valparaiso, near which he fell in with and captured a valuable Spanish ship, containing 60,000 pesos of gold, and 1770 jars of Chili wine; and soon after this, a still richer prize fell into his hands—the Cacafuego, with twenty-six tons of silver on board, thirteen chests of plate, and eighty pounds of gold. Drake now, dreading a capture of his treasures, resolved on

seeking a north-west passage homeward. In this
attempt, he reached the latitude of 42° north,
and attempted to find a passage to the eastward;
but failing in this, he steered westward for the
Cape of Good Hope, made the Philippines,
reached Java, doubled the Cape with comparative
ease, and on the 25th September, 1580, anchored
at Plymouth, having completed the circumnavi-
gation of the globe in two years and ten months.

The fame of his exploit and of the immense
booty he had acquired, soon rung throughout all
England. The queen, in April 1581, dined on
board his ship at Deptford, and conferred on its
commander the honour of knighthood. After
this, Sir Francis was made an admiral, in which
capacity he sailed in 1585, with an armament of
twenty-five ships, to the West Indies, and captured the cities of St. Jago, St. Domingo, and
Carthagena. Two years after, he attacked the
shipping in the bay of Cadiz, and burnt upwards
of 10,000 tons. In this expedition he also took
the St. Philip, a Portuguese caracca, from the
East Indies, with an immense treasure on board,
which capture is said to have suggested the first
idea of the establishment of our East India
Company.

In the following year he was appointed vice-
admiral, under Howard, earl of Effingham, and
acquitted himself most nobly in the attack on the

Spanish armada. In 1595, he was associated with Sir John Hawkins, on an expedition to the West Indies, during which he expired off Porto Bello, on the 28th January 1596.

### 32.—*Thomas Howard, Earl of Suffolk,*

Was the youngest son of Thomas, duke of Norfolk, beheaded in the reign of Elizabeth. He was created earl of Suffolk at the accession of James I.; soon afterwards, lord-chamberlain; and at length, lord-high-treasurer. He was convicted before the star-chamber of gross and corrupt peculation in his office, and other misdemeanors, for which he was dismissed, fined, and imprisoned.

### 33.—*Admiral Blake.*

Robert Blake was the son of a merchant at Bridgewater, in Somersetshire, where he was born, in August 1589. He was entered of Oxford university in 1615, where he took a degree. About 1640, he was returned by the puritan party for Bridgewater, and he served with the parliament army against Charles I.; but when the king was brought to trial, he condemned the measure as illegal. In 1648-9, being then sixty years of age, he was shifted from a military to a naval life, being appointed by Cromwell to command the fleet, in conjunction with Dean and Popham. He soon made himself formidable in his new capacity; blocked up prince Maurice and prince Rupert in Kinsale harbour, and afterwards following them from port to port, at last attacked them in that of Malaga, and nearly destroyed their whole fleet.

In 1652, Blake was appointed sole admiral, when his first exploit was to reduce the isle of Guernsey, which, until then, had held out for the king. In the ensuing year, the Dutch having declared against the commonwealth of England, he defeated their fleet, commanded by Van Tromp, Ruyter, and De Wit, in three several engagements, with great loss; and at length quite crippled their naval power, by a complete victory gained over them in June 1652, off Calais. In November 1654, he sailed with a strong fleet up the Mediterranean, and in December entered the road of Cadiz, where he was treated with all imaginable respect by the Dutch and French squadrons. The Algerines, too, conciliated his favour by presents and concessions, and most of the piratical states stood in awe of his name. The Dey of Tunis alone set him at defiance, refused all satisfaction for piracies committed on the English, and even denied Blake the liberty of taking in fresh water. " Here," said he, " are our castles of Goletta and Porto Ferino; do your worst." Blake, thus taunted, deliberately demolished these fortresses, and converting nine of the enemy's own vessels into fire-ships, destroyed their fleet in the harbour. This daring action rendered his name formidable throughout Africa and Asia; the governments of Malta and Tripoli made restitution of effects taken by their privateers from the English, and most of the states of Italy sent friendly embassies to Cromwell. The Spaniards too, had soon reason to stand in awe of the name of Blake, who chased and burnt their ships wherever he found them. Finding at length that the Spanish plate fleet had put into the bay of Santa Cruz, he weighed anchor, with twenty-five men-of-war, on the 13th April 1657: and on the 20th discovered sixteen Spanish ships in the bay, ranged in the form of a half-moon, defended by a strong castle, and seven forts, with a line of communication manned by musketeers. Notwithstanding these advantages, Blake burnt or sunk all the ships of the Spanish fleet, and by a fortunate change of wind came out without loss.

This was the admiral's last exploit: he was now nearly seventy years of age, and his constitution, weakened by hard service, yielded before a complicated attack of dropsy and scurvy. He sailed for England, and died as he was entering Plymouth sound, August 27, 1657.

He was, by Cromwell's order, buried with

great magnificence in Henry the Seventh's chapel, in Westminster abbey; whence, however, his body was pitifully expelled at the Restoration, and thrown into a pit in St. Margaret's churchyard.

## 34.—*Sir John Norris.*

A military leader of the reign of Elizabeth, who distinguished himself against the prince of Parma in the Low Countries, and subsequently in the unsuccessful attempt to place Don Antonio on the throne of Portugal.

## 35.—*Richard Bancroft, Archbishop of Canterbury.*

This prelate was born at Farnworth, Lancashire, in 1544, and studied at Cambridge, where he took his degrees of B. A., M. A., and D. D. After several gradations of church preferment, he was, in 1597, made chaplain to archbishop Whitgift, and in the same year appointed bishop of London. In 1600, he was sent by queen Elizabeth to settle some differences between the English and the Danes. He also strongly supported the secular priests against the jesuits; which, together with his violent invectives against the puritans, obtained him the favour of the church party, and his promotion to the see of London.

Bancroft enjoyed queen Elizabeth's favour, and attended her during her last illness. At the commencement of James's reign, he was one of the chief commissioners on behalf of the church, at the famous Hampton-court conference between the bishops and the presbyterian ministers, and took a leading part in the disputations. On the death of Whitgift, in 1603, Bancroft was advanced to the see of Canterbury, and in 1610, he succeeded the earl of Dorset as chancellor of Oxford. He died in 1612, at Lambeth palace, and left his library to his successors for ever. He was a strict disciplinarian, a powerful preacher and speaker, of high moral courage, and possessed of sound and extensive learning.

### 36.—*William, first Prince of Orange,*

Was born about the year 1533. He was among the first to head the insurrection in the Low Countries, which eventually succeeded in throwing off the yoke of the Spanish government. He fell by the hand of an assassin, in 1584, said to have been instigated to the deed by the court of Spain.

## 37.—*Thomas Ratcliff, Earl of Sussex,*

The son of Henry Ratcliff, earl of Sussex, a general in the army of queen Mary. The son is not prominent in English history; the chief public events in which he distinguished himself being, first, the negociation of the marriage articles between queen Elizabeth and John of Austria, which is supposed to have been mere illusion, to conceal other projects; and secondly, when he had the command of the English army against the Scots. This nobleman, however, was remarkable for political ability and penetration, as well as for military talent; and there is reason to believe that his opinions had great weight with the queen's council, in many very important events. Many of his letters are preserved in the various collections, in which he advises on measures connected with Scotland, France, and the Low Countries.

## 38.—*Sir Walter Mildmay, Knt.*

Was a younger son of Thomas Mildmay, esq., of Moulsham, Essex, educated at Christ's college, Cambridge, and became chancellor of the Exchequer in the reign of Elizabeth. He was eminent in literature, and a patron of learning.

Emanuel college, Cambridge, was founded by him, and he conferred donations on Christ's-college. He died in 1589.

## 39.—*Erasmus.*

This celebrated writer was born at Rotterdam, in 1467. He published an edition of the New Testament in 1516, being the first time it was printed in Greek, and many learned works, philological and religious. He died at Basil in 1536, and was buried in the cathedral there. He is generally considered to have been the most learned man of the age in which he lived; and he certainly contributed, both by his example and his writings, to the revival of literature in Europe.

## 40.—*Isabella of the Low Countries.*

Isabella Clara Eugenia, governess of the Netherlands, was the daughter of Philip II. of Spain, and of his second wife, Elizabeth, daughter of Henry II. of France. During the life-time of Philip, she was contracted to Albert, archduke of Austria, son of the emperor Maximilian, and appointed to the government of the Low Countries. The marriage was solemnized, and the appointment confirmed, shortly after the accession of Philip III; and they made a sumptuous entry into Brussels, in September 1599, when the mag-

2 E

nificence of their court, and the adoption of Spanish manners, occasioned some dissatisfaction. To Albert was entrusted the conduct of the war against the Dutch, commanded by Prince Maurice. On one occasion, the troops having been ordered to assemble at Bruges, in order to march against the Dutch, some murmurs arose respecting the irregularity of their pay. As they passed near Ghent, Isabella, mounted on horseback, went out to meet and harangue them, and as they complained of the above-mentioned circumstance, she declared, that rather than their demands should not be satisfied, she would expose to sale her plate and jewels, and deliver up to them the funds appropriated to the support of her court and servants. Albert, at the same time putting himself at their head, declared he would share their fortunes. The appeal was successful, and the battle of Minport, fought July 1600, against the Dutch, followed, in which, however, Albert was defeated and wounded. This battle decided the independence of Holland, though the war still continued. Albert next laid seige to Ostend, which he took after more than one hundred thousand men on both sides had been sacrificed. A truce was concluded in 1609 for twelve years, before the expiration of which Albert died, in 1629. Isabella appears to have been a woman of masculine spirit, but her government was mild, and she was much beloved.

## 41.—*Melancthon and Pomeranus.*

Melancthon, a fellow-labourer, and attached friend of Luther's, was Greek professor at the university of Wittenberg. Pomeranus was also a contributor to the great work of the Reformation, and was one who assisted in the translation of the Scriptures. *

## 42.—*John Huss, Reformer and Martyr,*

Was born at Huss, in Bohemia. He became professor of divinity in the university of Prague, and pastor of the church in that city; and was distinguished for remarkable erudition and eloquence. He adopted the sentiments of Wickliffe; and about 1407, began to preach openly against the corruptions of the church, and the flagrant errors of the sacerdotal order. The resentment of the clergy was soon inflamed against him; but Huss persevered in recommending the writings and opinions of Wickliffe, and in denouncing the despotism of the church of Rome. In 1410, sentence of excommunication was passed against him; after which, as he still boldly persisted in the promulgation of his tenets, he was summoned to appear before the council of Constance. The emperor Sigismund guaranteed him safe conduct to and from the council, and he therefore did not hesitate to appear before it; but, by a most scandalous breach of faith, the promise of safe conduct was disregarded, he was cast into prisón by the council, declared a heretic, and burnt alive in 1415. He endured his fate with extraordinary magnanimity and firmness. His writings were burnt with him; but copies of most of them were preserved, and afterwards publishéd. His followers, after his death, broke out into open war, which lasted for many years, with horrible barbarities on both sides.

### 43.—*Rodolphus Agricola,*

Was one of the most learned scholars of the fifteenth century, and the immediate forerunner and prototype of the great Erasmus. He was born near Groningen, in Friesland, in 1443, and died in 1485, aged forty-two, leaving many works on classical literature, far superior to those of any of his contemporaries. He was, besides, a skilful practitioner of music and painting. He did not interfere towards the Reformation; but he seems to have foreseen that a crisis was approaching.

## 44.—*The Duke of Alvarez.*

Of whom we can find nothing, unless he was the Portuguese traveller of that name, who died in 1540.

## 45.—*Ninon de L'Enclos.*

Ninon de L'Enclos was born in 1616, and was the only child of a gentleman of Touraine, of a noble but not rich family. Her father, a professed philosopher of the epicurean school, early instilled in his daughter the principles which he had made the rule of his own life; thus preparing her to be what she afterwards became: his last words to her were, " be more scrupulous in the choice than in the number of your pleasures." Left an orphan at an early age, with a moderate independence, she came to Paris, and purchased a house, which became the resort of the most distinguished personages, of both sexes. " The only house," says a contemporary writer, " where the guests dared depend on their talents and acquirements, and where whole days could be passed without gambling and without ennui." The house was in the Rue des Tournelles, quartier de Marne, then the most fashionable part of the capital, and where the hotels of some of the most distinguished nobility of the court of Louis XIV. were situated. The hotel of Ninon (inhabited in 1830 by Signor Barbieri), is still in perfect preservation, and is ornamented with allegorical devices, supposed to be the work of Mignard and le Brun. In this house she resided sixty years, and here she died when ninety years of age. The house must be an object of interest to all who think of the illustrious personages who visited it. Amongst many other objects which attract attention, the spot is traditionally pointed out where Molière read to her many of his most celebrated pieces.

Though the fortune of Ninon was moderate, she rejected every offer of splendid dependance, even from royal power and devoted friendship. Madame de Maintenon made her repeated offers of liberal provision, which she declined. Christina of Sweden was so unwilling to part with her, that she used every means to prevail on Ninon to accompany her to Rome and reside in her palace; but Ninon preferred her house and society in the Rue des Tournelles. That she was disinterested and honourable, is proved by the following anecdotes. She was found at her toilet by the noblest of her lovers, curling her hair with the contract of marriage and bond for four thousand louis, which he had given her the night before; " Cela doit vous faire voir," said she to him, " quel cas je fais des promesses de jeunes étourdis comme vous, et combien vous vous compromettriez avec une femme capable de profiter de vos folies." When de Gourville was driven into exile, he left with her one half of his fortune : the other half he confided to the grand penitencier, who, on the return of Gourville, affected to have forgotten the transaction, and threatened his friend with unpleasant consequences should he persist in his demand. Deceived by the churchman, he did not think of applying to Ninon, who he imagined more likely to have spent his money. She sent for him, and when they met, said, " I have to reproach myself deeply on your account ; a great misfortune has happened to me during your absence, for which I have to solicit your pardon." Gourville thought this of course related to his deposit. " I have lost the inclination I had for you," continued she, " but I have not lost my memory ; here are the twenty thousand crowns you entrusted to my care ; take the casket in which they are, and let us live for the future as friends."

This extraordinary woman retained her charms to an advanced period of life. At fifty-seven years of age she made the conquest of the marquis de Sevigné, so humourously immortalized by his mother ; she was upwards of sixty when the chevalier de Villiers fell upon his sword, on discovering the object of his passion to be *his mother;* at seventy, she achieved the conquest of the baron de Bernier, of the royal family of Sweden, and at eighty that of the abbé Gedoyn, a young jesuit.

St. Evremond says of her,—

> " L'indulgente et sage nature
> A formee l'ame de Ninon
> De la volupte d'epicure,
> Et de la vertu de Caton."

She was good-tempered, liberal, witty, and highly accomplished ; and old age found her in possession of all that had rendered her faults endurable—her benevolence, her philosophy and her intellect. " If," she was wont to say, " one could believe that in dying one was going to talk with old friends, it would be sweet to die." In the last hour of her struggle with life, she composed the following lines :—

> " Qu'un vain espoire ne vienne pas offrir,
> Qui puisse ebranler mon courage;
> Je suis en age de mourir,
> Que ferais-je ici d'avantage ?"

Some of Ninon's letters to St. Evremond, which are found in the works of that author, and have been published separately in the " Lettres des Femmes Célébres," are the only authentic memorials of her pen.

### 46.—*The Countess of Desmond.*

Another veteran beauty, who lived to upwards of one hundred years of age. She was the wife of the once-potent Irish earl of Desmond, who sided with the Yorkists during the contentions of the houses of York and Lancaster, and lost an enormous property in the cause.

### 47.—*Luther.*

Martin Luther, one of the most intrepid and successful of religious reformers, was the son of a German miner, and born at Eisteben, in Saxony, Nov. 10th, 1484. He was educated for the law; but he suddenly became an Augustine friar, and was for a time distinguished by his zeal for the Roman Catholic faith. A tour which he made to Rome, in 1510, first opened his eyes to the corruptions of that church; and the writings of Huss added further conviction. In 1512, being then professor of divinity in the university of Wittemberg, he began to propagate his new opinions in his public lectures; and, as he possessed an ardent imagination, considerable eloquence, and, above all, a purity of character in strict accordance with his doctrines, his audiences were soon large and influential. A host of opponents, of

2 F

course, rose against him, by whom he was denounced as a heretic ; but he went fearlessly forward, discussing the subjects of indulgences, the sacraments, laws divine and human, the nature of vows, &c.

The court of Rome at first treated the whole matter with contempt ; but at length, finding that the new doctrines were really becoming popular, Luther was summoned by pope Leo X. to appear before him. On the interposition, however, of the elector of Saxony, the matter was referred to cardinal Cajetan, the pope's legate at Augsburg, who required a recantation of all that had been promulgated. To this, Luther would not submit, and he was, therefore, advised by his friends to withdraw from Augsburg to Wittemberg. This he consented to; but, before his departure he appealed, first to the pope, and then to a general council. Incensed at this, Cajetan called upon the elector to deliver him up; but Frederick declined submitting to this injunction, and the death of the emperor Maximilian at this juncture, fortunately turned, for a time, the attention of Luther's enemies to another object. In the meantime our reformer, nothing daunted, had begun to express doubts of the divine origin of the pope's authority, and of the legality of the wealth and power of the clergy. The pope now, on the 15th June, 1520, passed sentence of excommunication against him as a heretic. Luther again appealed, denounced the pope and his tyranny, threw the book of the canon-law, and the bull of excommunication into the flames, and harangued a great multitude of spectators on the mischievous and wicked tendency of the papal doctrines.

The diet of Worms was now called on, through Charles V., the new emperor, forthwith to condemn Luther to death; but they refused to do this without first examining him, and sent to require his appearance, all the princes through whose territories he was to pass, promising him a safe conduct. Luther, contrary to the advice of his friends, determined to go. He was received at Worms, by princes, nobles, and persons of all ranks, with distinguished marks of respect. When before the diet, he refused to renounce his opinions; and he was allowed to leave the city in safety, but had not long quitted it, before a decree was issued, pronouncing him an obstinate heretic, depriving him of all his rights as a subject, and calling upon every one to seize him. His situation now became most critical; but he was preserved by a stratagem, suggested by his kind friend, the elector of Saxony. Near Altenstrain, he was suddenly surrounded by a body of horsemen in masks, who, dismissing his attendants, carried him off to the castle of Wortburg. Here he lay concealed for nine months; and here he first prepared his greatest and most useful work—the translation of the Scriptures into the German language. He first published the Gospels of Matthew and Mark: these were followed by the Epistle to the Romans; and about the end of September 1522, the entire New Testament was in circulation. He next proceeded with the Old Testament, which was completed in 1530. He was now at open war with the pope and the clergy, whom he designated in his works as tyrants and impious persons, and his doctrines continued to advance, in spite of numerous papal edicts issued against him and his disciples.

About the end of the year 1524, Luther resigned his monk's gown, and in June 1525, he married. He was most happy in this union, and continued still to be as zealously active as ever in the great cause. The Reformation had now taken deep root; and Luther's chief solicitude was, to exhort and advise the princes and states that had adopted his doctrines, and to publish such works as might confute his opponents, and encourage his friends. In 1535, his version of the Bible, in German, was first published.

About 1538, pope Pius III., finding that protestants could not be compelled to retract their opinions, began to talk of a reform of the church. This was ridiculed by Luther, who continued to write against the prevalent corruptions with unflinching intrepidity and perseverance, until his death, which happened in the year 1546. He was interred with high honours : princes, nobles, and students attended the procession, and the funeral oration was delivered by his attached friend and fellow-labourer, Melancthon.

Luther reduced the number of sacraments to two ; he also exploded the adoration of the host, auricular confession, indulgences, purgatory, the worship of images, the Romish fasts, monastic vows, the celibacy of the clergy, and other errors of the church of Rome.

### 48.—*Philip, Count de Horne;*

One of the leaders of the insurrection in the Low Countries against the oppressive government of the Spaniards. The contest occupied the arms of Spain for nearly half a century, and was in the end successful ; but the count de Horne and count Egmont falling into the hands of the unrelenting duke of Alva, were put to death in an early part of the struggle.

### 49.—*Lord George Sackville—afterwards, Sackville-Germaine—and eventually, Viscount Sackville.*

This nobleman, of somewhat unfortunate reputation in his day, was named after his godfather, king

George I. He was educated at Westminster and
the university of Dublin. In 1737, he entered
the army ; and in 1740, was lieutenant-colonel of
the 28th foot. He was at the battles of Dettingen
and Fontenoy, and is admitted to have signalized
himself in both. He also served with the duke of
Cumberland in Scotland, during the rebellion of
1745 and 46, and abroad in 47–48. In 1749, he
was promoted to the colonelcy of the 12th dragoons,
and soon after to the command of the horse-cari-
bineers in Ireland. He became major-general in
1755 ; colonel of the 2nd dragoon-guards and
lieutenant-general of the ordnance in 1757 ; and
soon afterwards lieutenant-general of his majesty's
forces, and a member of the privy-council. For
some time he commanded a division of the army
encamped near Chatham, and it is related of him
that, being solicited by the celebrated Whitfield
for permission to address the soldiers, he acceded
to the request, by the following laconic reply :
" Tell the gentleman from me, that he may preach
anything he pleases to them that is not against the
articles of war."

In 1759, on the death of the duke of Marlborough, Lord George Sackville succeeded him in
the command of the British forces in Germany,
under prince Frederick of Brunswick, generalissimo of the allied army in the pay of Great
Britain, and was placed at the head of the cavalry

in the battle of Minden. During the action, the allied infantry having thrown the enemy into some disorder, prince Ferdinand sent orders for Lord George to advance; but his instructions were misunderstood, and the cavalry did not come in for any share of the action. The next day, in the general orders issued by the commander-in-chief, Lord George was by implication deeply censured. He immediately returned to England, where he was at once ignominiously dismissed from all his employments. He demanded a court-martial, the sentence of which was, that he was " unfit for military command." This sentence was confirmed by the king, who moreover ordered the name of lord George Sackville to be struck out of the list of privy-councillors. Nevertheless, it is difficult to believe in the justice of the sentence, which many persons, even at that time, did not hesitate to stigmatise as iniquitous. Anything like proof of cowardice was certainly never established; indeed the evidence would rather substantiate an accusation of rashness, and his lordship's previous military services, during which he had on several occasions so distinguished himself as to cause his rapid promotion, would seem to be an answer to so base a charge as that of holding back through fear. That the prince's order to advance, however, was not *obeyed*, is certain; the answer to which is, that not having been sufficiently precise to be intelligible, it was not intentionally disobeyed. It is now generally believed, that lord George Sackville was treated harshly by his brother officers, either to gratify a pique of prince Ferdinand's, from party spirit, which ran high at the time, or from other motives now inscrutable. One of the first acts of king George III., after his accession, was to recal lord George to court ;* which step, taken at a period when the whole case was fresh in the public memory, must certainly be considered as a virtual repeal of a verdict delivered only a few months before.

In 1761, his lordship was returned to parliament for Hythe, in Kent. In 1770, he succeeded to considerable property under the will of his aunt, lady Betty Germaine, and he then took the name of Germaine, in accordance with her desire. He had previously been elected M. P. for East Grinstead, which he represented from 1768 until 1782. In 1775, he was admitted into the administration, and was, in succession, joint vice-treasurer of Ireland, first lord of trade and plantations, and secretary of state for the colonies. In this latter capacity, he strenuously supported the American war. On the dissolution of the administration of which he was a member, he was raised to the peerage by the title of viscount Sack-

* See North Britain, No. 45.

ville and baron Bolebroke. On his taking his seat among the peers, the Minden affair was again brought forward, and a motion made that his lordship's elevation " was an insufferable indignity to that house." On a division, however, it was rejected by ninety-three to twenty-eight votes.

His lordship was not distinguished by extraordinary ability, but he was a powerful speaker, and took a decided and conspicuous part in parliament on several occasions, with great plausibility and address. He is supposed to have owed his elevation to the zeal with which he supported the contest with America. Of his speaking, a contemporary says, " his manner is peculiar; his style nervous and manly; his language elegance itself; and his observations pointed, sententious, and convincing." He has been named amongst the supposed authors of Junius; but this was denied by himself, and there is little to favour the supposition.

His lordship married Diana, second daughter and co-heir of John Sambroke, esq. He died in 1785.

## 50.—*Miss Stewart.*

Frances Theresa Stewart was the elder of two daughters of Walter, lord Blantyre, a peer of Scotland. Immediately on her introduction at

court, she became maid of honour to Catherine of
Braganza, and the darling intimate of the countess
of Castlemain, afterwards duchess of Cleveland,
who endeavoured, by strange artifices, to inspire
the king with a passion for her, in order, as con-
jectured by Grammont, to turn attention from her
own amours, or to prevent his forming an attachment to others more likely to interfere with her
views. The king became violently enamoured;
the young lady repelled his attacks on her honour,
and Charles is supposed to have felt a real attachment for her. This passion led him into several
singular, but inoffensive extravagances; among
these, a gold medal appeared, doubtless by his
order, representing on the front his own bust,
and on the reverse a portrait of the idolized fair
in the character of Minerva. This figure was
soon afterwards transferred to the copper coin of
the realm, on which it now appears, unaltered in
general appearance, as the emblematical figure
and bearing the inscription of Britannia. A
rumour gained credit, that Charles intended to
divorce his queen and marry this lady; who, in
order to preserve her reputation and avoid the
king's importunities, encouraged the honourable
addresses of Charles Lenox, duke of Richmond,
to whom she was married in 1669, having left
Whitehall privately after much opposition and vex-
ation. Clarendon fell under the displeasure of

Charles, for having, as his enemies informed the
king, contributed to this marriage. The duchess
of Richmond survived her husband, who left her
childless, and having remained a widow thirty
years, died in 1702, possessed of considerable
wealth, which she bequeathed to her great nephew,
Alexander, fifth lord Blantyre.

## 51.—*Countess of Shrewsbury.*

Anna Maria, daughter of Robert Brudenel,
second earl of Cardigan, wife of Francis Talbot,
eleventh earl of Shrewsbury. Her husband was
killed in a duel with her paramour, George
Villiers, second Duke of Buckingham. She is
said to have held the duke's horse, in the disguise
of a page, while he shed her husband's life-blood;
and other circumstances are related of her conduct
immediately after the combat, too horrible and
disgusting to be repeated. The orphan earl, who
was born in 1666, received his name from his
sponsor, Charles II. He was seven years of age
at the time of his father's death.

During the minority of himself and brother,
a petition was presented to the king, imploring
justice on Buckingham, touching smartly upon
the duke's scandalous behaviour, and bitterly
complaining that, after having basely murdered
their father, he continued to load the family with

reproach, at a time when the successors to the honour and family of Shrewsbury, being yet infants, were not able to do themselves justice on the person who had so notoriously injured them. It does not appear that the remonstrance produced any effect. The elder son became a favourite with William III.

## 52.—*Major Mohun.*

This singular portrait, the artist of which is not known, represents a man in his shirt, with a sword in his hand, apparently in the act of defending himself. Mohun was a comedian in the reign of Charles I., and, on the breaking out of the civil wars, became a volunteer in the royal army, and distinguished himself on several occasions.

## 53.—*Sir Kenelm Digby.*

This is one of the finest portraits, if not *the* finest in the collection at Knole.

Sir Kenelm Digby was the son of Sir Everard Digby, who was beheaded for his participation in the gunpowder plot. The son became eminent both as an author and a statesman. His life was eventful: king Charles I. made him a gentleman of the bedchamber, commissioner of the navy, and governor of the Trinity-house ; and subsequently granted him letters of reprisals against the Venetians, by virtue of which he, with a very inconsiderable fleet, took several prizes, and fighting his way through the enemy with great gallantry, came clear off with his booty.

During the civil wars, he was one of the most faithful adherents of the royal cause, and was in consequence compelled to compound his estate and become an exile, during Cromwell's usurpation. He retired to France, and was sent on two embassies to pope Innocent X., from the widowed queen of Charles I., to whom he was chancellor. He returned to England in 1661, and was appointed one of the council on the first institution of the royal society. He died in London in 1665. He was the author of several learned works, and a great benefactor to the Bodleian library, by presenting it, in 1663, with a large collection of manuscripts. He translated various authors into English ; and his treatise on the Nature of Bodies and the Immortality of the Soul, is thought to evince extraordinary knowledge and penetration.

## 54.—*Du Burg, Organist of Antwerp.*

We regret to state that we cannot find any account of this musician. There were several Du Burgs of some eminence, both as performers and com-

posers, but we cannot identify either of them
with the " organist of Antwerp." There is probably some mistake in the description of the
portrait, an etching from which, or from a painting like it, by Vandyke, has been seen with the
following inscription under it : "Henricus Liberti,
organist of Antwerp cathedral."

## 55.—*Anne Carr, Countess of Bedford,*

The daughter of Robert Carr, earl of Somerset,
and Frances, daughter of Thomas Howard, first
earl of Suffolk. At the age of seventeen she
was married to William, lord Russel, son and heir
of Francis, fourth earl of Bedford, after many
objections and delays on the part of the earl.
Seven sons and four daughters were the issue of
this union, which was one of affection, and proved
happy. She died in 1684, oppressed with grief
for the loss of her second son, lord William
Russel, executed for treason in 1683.

## 56.—*Sir Ralph Bosville, Knt.*

Formerly of Bradborne, near Sevenoaks, where
the family lived for several generations. Their
estates have now passed into other hands ; Mr.
Ralph Bosville, a lineal descendant of the knight,
having, by his will, passed over all his relatives,
and left his property to Mr., afterwards Sir

Richard, Bettison, for life (who, in the capacity of clerk in the South-sea House, had shown him some civilities).; and in the event of his dying without male issue, which he did, to the family of the Lanes, of Sevenoaks.

## 57.—*Sir Hatton Fermor, Knt.*

One of the ancestors of the noble family of Pomfret, was the son of Sir George Fermor, of Easton, in Northamptonshire, and sheriff of that county in 1618. Sir George had the honour of entertaining king James I. and his queen, at Easton, on the 11th June 1603; on which occasion his majesty knighted Sir Hatton, his eldest son.

## 58.—*Henry Howard, Earl of Surrey,*

The eldest son of the third duke of Norfolk, was born about 1516, and educated in Windsor castle, with young Fitzroy, earl of Richmond, natural son of king Henry VIII. About 1532, he was affianced, and soon afterwards married, to the lady Frances Vere, daughter of the earl of Oxford. Shortly after this, he was one of those who attended the king into France, to the " Field of the Cloth of Gold." In 1533, he bore a part in the coronation of his cousin, Ann Boleyn ; and three.

years after, it is melancholy to find him sitting as
earl-marshal, in his father's stead, at the trial and
condemnation of the young queen.

At about this period of his life commenced an
attachment to a lady, by some thought to have
been platonic only, which has given rise to a ro-
mantic tale of the earl of Surrey's making an expedition into Italy, in the principal cities of
which kingdom, in various tournaments, he maintained the fair Geraldine's superlative beauty
" against all comers, whether Christians, Jews,
Saracens, Turks, or Cannibals," and was victorious in them all; as well as in one fought at
Westminster, in 1540. For this fanciful story,
there seems but slight foundation. Surrey unquestionably conceived an attachment for the fair
Geraldine, who was a daughter of the earl of
Kildare, and is described as the greatest beauty of
her time. This lady he has immortalised in his
sonnets; but he himself makes no mention of
having tilted in her honour, or visited foreign
lands to celebrate her beauty. At the period,
too, when these feats are said to have been performed, Surrey himself appears to have been in
England, and the lady was not more than ten or
eleven years of age. This knight-errant expedition, therefore, must be regarded as an absurd
fiction. It should be added, in justice to the earl,
who was a married man at the time, that he lived

in perfect harmony with his wife, and always sustained a high moral character.

In 1543, the earl of Surrey went as a volunteer in the armament against France, under the command of Sir John Wallop, and distinguished himself so conspicuously, that, in 1544, he was appointed marshal of the army, at the head of which king Henry VIII. invaded France in person. Surrey ably seconded the duke, his father, in an attempt to reduce Montreuil, and was dangerously wounded. From want of ammunition and provision, however, they were compelled to raise the siege; and as merit is too commonly estimated by success, this failure, though all was done that skill or valour could accomplish, seems to have incurred the king's displeasure. Notwithstanding this, he was, in 1546, made captain-general of the English forces in France, where he displayed so much courage, energy, and skill, as to acquire the reputation of one of the ablest soldiers of the day. He several times defeated the French, with inferior forces; but being, on one occasion, worsted in an attempt to intercept a convoy, he was recalled to England, and superseded by the earl of Hertford.

After the death of his wife, Surrey had the boldness to propose himself to the princess Mary. For this the Seymours, rivals of the Norfolk family, and favourites with the king, accused him

2 H

of aspiring to the crown. Accordingly, Surrey and his father were, on the 12th Dec., 1546, committed to the Tower; and on the 13th January following, Surrey was tried and convicted at Guildhall, and beheaded on Tower-hill on the 19th, in the thirtieth year of his age, only nine days before the death of the king. The accusations brought against this amiable young nobleman on his trial, were so inane and trivial, that it seems miraculous how any judge and jury could be found so villainous as to carry on the farce of justice. The chief accusation against him was, that he had quartered with his own the arms of Edward the Confessor: and for this assumption, for which he had the authority of the heralds' college, was consigned to an untimely grave the most gallant and accomplished gentleman of the age, whether as soldier, courtier, or poet. His poems, which are replete with nature and feeling, of graceful fancy, and undeniable good taste, were several times printed in the reign of Elizabeth and James. An edition was published in 1824, edited by G. F. Nott, and another in 1832, in Pickering's " Aldine Poets."

## 60.—Sir Anthony Cope, Bart.

There have been several baronets of this family of the same name, all of them ancestors of the late duchess of Dorset. Of these, the first and the most distinguished, was Sir Anthony, vice-chamberlain to queen Catherine Parr, and one of the most learned men of the era in which he lived. His only daughter, Ann, became the wife of Sir Kenelm Digby. We believe, however, that this portrait represents Sir Anthony Cope, of Hanwell, who was created a baronet by king James I., in 1611. He was high-sheriff of Oxford, and M. P. for Banbury.

## 61.—*Anthony Ashley Cooper, Earl of Shaftesbury.*

This celebrated statesman was the son of Sir John Cooper, of Rockburn, Hants, and born in 1621. He was entered of Exeter college, Oxford, and thence removed to Lincoln's-inn, for the study of the law. At the age of nineteen, he sat in parliament as member for Tewkesbury.

On the breaking out of the civil wars, young Cooper first attached himself to the king's party; but he suddenly shifted over to the popular side, in a manner which, from whatever cause it may have arisen, it seems impossible to reconcile with integrity. About 1646, he succeeded to his father's baronetcy, and became sheriff of Wilts. On the dissolution of the long parliament, Sir Anthony was appointed one of the members of the convention; and for some years after this, he, opposed and protested against the arbitrary measures of Cromwell on several occasions, with most laudable independence and boldness. After the protectorate, he took part with Monk in the measures which led to the Restoration, and was one of the twelve who carried the invitation to Charles II. On the arrival of that king, he was appointed a member of the privy-council, and (what is but little creditable to his political memory) he accepted the office of commissioner for the trial of the regicides, his former partisans.

In 1661, Sir Anthony was created baron Ashley; and soon after, chancellor and under-treasurer of the Exchequer, and a commissioner of the Treasury. His public conduct for the ensuing ten years has been variously represented by party-writers, whose testimony is so conflicting, that it is now wholly impossible to come to a correct conclusion. That he was a leading member of the famous (or infamous) cabal ministry, is certain, and the plan of shutting up the Exchequer is strongly imputed to him; but, on the other hand, he appears to have been strenuous and sincere in promoting religious toleration, and his sentiments, as recorded in his speeches, are independent and manly.

In 1672, his lordship was raised to an earldom, by the title of baron Cooper and earl of Shaftesbury; and in November of the same year, he was made lord-chancellor. In this office, however, he was superseded, in less than two years, by Sir Heneage Finch: and from this period the earl of Shaftesbury is again found in the ranks of the opposition, and, with the exception of a few months, during which he was lord-president of the council, he continued out of office during the remainder of his life. He retired from party-strife in 1682, and embarked for Holland, where he purposed to reside, and had just completed a suitable establishment at Amsterdam, when he died of gout, on the 22nd January, 1683.

The political character of this nobleman is, to say the least of it, equivocal. His tergiversation is proved, on more than one occasion, to have arisen from interested motives; and the charge of being factious as well as selfish, seems to have been fully substantiated: yet it is difficult to believe all that his biographers have urged against him. As lord-chancellor, during the short time that he held the seals, his conduct was most able and impartial.

## 62.—*Catherine II. of Russia.*

Catherine II. of Russia was the daughter of the prince of Anhalt Zerbst, governor of Stettin, in Prussian Pomerania, at which place she was born in 1729. In 1745, she married her cousin, Charles-Frederic, Duke of Holstein. His aunt, Elizabeth, empress of Russia, having chosen him her successor, he was declared grand-duke of Russia, and took the name of Peter III. They were ill-assorted ; Catherine, handsome, fond of pleasure, ambitious and bold, could ill brook the fondness of Peter for his Holstein guards, his inclination to low pleasures, his mistress the countess Vrontzoff Passick, his imprudence and want of resolution. The marriage was consequently unhappy, and on the death of the empress Elizabeth, when Peter ascended the throne of Russia, he wished to repudiate his wife, who was living at Peterhop, a country residence not far from Petersburg. Catherine and her friends determined to anticipate his designs ; a confederacy was formed in her favour, and several regiments of the guards were gained over, when the whole was discovered by the indiscretion of an officer, who by mistake gave some order to a person not entrusted with the secret, who immediately caused him to be put under arrest. Previous, however, to his confinement, he contrived to write on a slip of paper, " all is discovered, lose no time :" the paper reached Gregory Orloff, who, repairing to the barracks, sent his brother Alexius to the empress, whilst he endeavoured to prepare for her reception at Petersburg. On his arrival,

Alexius went to Monplaisir, a small summer-house, of which his brother had given him the key, with instructions how to gain admission. Catherine, who had long retired to rest, was startled, at two o'clock in the morning, by the appearance of a person in a military habit, who only said, " get ready to follow me," and disap-peared. Catherine obeyed the summons ; Alexius was in waiting, and led her through a private gate to a carriage, which had been engaged some days previous by the princess Dashkof for a party of pleasure. The empress entered it, and Alexius, taking the reins, drove off with all possible expe-dition. Long before the end of their journey the carriage became unfit to proceed, and they were continuing their journey on foot when a light cart fortunately coming up, they got into it and Alexius again drove on. They soon after met Gregory Orloff, who, anxious at the delay occa-sioned by the accident, came to seek them. Finding all safe, he returned to Petersburg, where Catherine arrived early in the morning. Finding all prepared, she dressed herself in the uniform of a young officer named Taliezen, and, mounting on horseback, showed herself at the head of the troops. It was at this time that Potemkin, after-wards a chief favourite, but then only an officer in the guards, perceiving the empress had no plume in her cap, detached his own and presented it :

he also contrived to ride by her side, and thus gave her an opportunity of remarking the beauty of his person. Catherine was declared sole empress, and when Peter at length arrived, he was arrested, deposed, imprisoned, and forced to sign an act of abdication. Six days after this, the conspirators, fearing a reaction among the troops, despatched Alexius Orloff and another to Ropscha, where Peter was confined. They conversed cheerfully with him, giving him hopes of soon being at liberty, and drinking with him, as was the custom before dinner, they infused poison into the liquor. Other accounts say that he was strangled : probably strangulation might be resorted to in order to hasten his end, but his body when laid in state exhibited evident marks of poison. It does not appear that Catherine actually ordered the murder, but she showed no surprise at it, and continued her favour to the perpetrators.

The events in the life of Catherine have been related by many authors. Among those of a political nature may be mentioned the troubles in Poland, which led to a war with Turkey (in which the Russian armies were generally victorious), and ultimately, in 1795, to the third and last division of Poland between Austria, Prussia, and Russia ; and her journey to the Crimea, which the Russians had taken to themselves, and which took place in 1785, in a style which resembled a triumphal procession. She reformed the laws of Russia, ameliorated the condition of the serfs, established schools for youth, and for the study of medicine, languages, &c., throughout the kingdom, favoured commerce and manufactures, and employed learned men to visit the remotest parts of her empire, and to correspond with the French literati. Her attention to the education of her grandchildren has been often dwelt on, and her treatment of her favourites (among the chief of whom were Orloff and Potemkin) may be likewise mentioned. She reigned sole empress thirty-five years, and died of apoplexy, 17th November, 1796, aged sixty-seven.

### 63.—*Miss Axford.*

The fair quakeress, who was noticed by king George III. when Prince of Wales.

### 64.—*Sir John Suckling,*

A spirited dramatist, and travelled man of fashion of the seventeenth century, was born at Witham, in Essex. He was remarkable in his youth for quickness of intellect, and his early acquirements in school-learning are admitted to have been extraordinary. Before he was twenty years of age, he had travelled over a great portion of civilized Europe; and in the course of his tour he became a soldier, and served in a short but active campaign under the celebrated Gustavus Adolphus. On his return to England, he was received as the " admired of all admirers," a wit, a courtier, and a fine gentleman. He died at an early age (about thirty), and appears to have led a busy yet careless life, sometimes writing verses, at others gambling or dying of love: now raising a troop of soldiers for the king, and soon after plotting with the cavaliers. His chief vice was gaming.*

## 65.—*Ann, Countess of Dorset, Pembroke, and Montgomery.*

This lady was the celebrated Anne Clifford, daughter of George Clifford, earl of Cumberland.* She was married, in 1609, to Richard, third earl of Dorset, by whom she had five children; all of whom, however, except one daughter, who married a Tufton, an ancestor of the present earl of Thanet, died in their infancy. The earl of Dorset himself died in his thirty-fifth year. After his decease, his lady formed a second ma-

* For a notice of his literary productions, see Retrospective Review, vols. ix and x.

† See Appendix, No. 15.

trimonial connexion with Philip, earl of Pembroke and Montgomery, whom she also survived.

The literary acquirements of this lady were so conspicuous, that Walpole has assigned her a place among the " royal and noble authors." She was also noted for active beneficence, and a life of usefulness ; in the course of which she built two hospitals, and erected or repaired seven churches. She also erected monuments to the poets Spenser and Daniels, the latter of whom was her tutor. She is particularly celebrated for a spirited reply to Sir Joseph Williamson, secretary of state to king Charles II. He had presumed to nominate a candidate for *her* borough of Appleby, when she addressed him in the following laconic and determined style :—" I have been bullied by an usurper ; I have been neglected by a court ; but I will not be dictated to by a subject : your man sha'nt stand."

## 66.—*Monsieur Campchinetz.*

This gentleman was an officer in the Swiss guards, when they were overpowered by the revolutionists in the Thuilleries. He lay concealed among the dead soldiers till night afforded him an opportunity to escape. Being conversant with the English language, he represented himself as an

Englishman, and, disguising himself as a servant, lived for some years as ostler at an inn in France, until at length he contrived to escape to England. He was a frequent visitor at Knole House.

## 67.—*Count Ugolino.*

Conte Ugolino de Gherardeschi di Pisa, after having rendered himself master of Pisa by the assistance of Roger (archbishop of Pisa), of the Ubaldini family, and treacherously deprived his nephew, Ninodi Galluva, of the supreme command, was himself betrayed by the archbishop, who caused the Pisans to believe Ugolino had delivered some of their castles into the hands of the Florentines. The unfortunate count was decoyed into a tower, with two of his sons and two nephews, and having been kept there from August to March, they were at last left to perish with hunger. Dante, in the thirty-third canto of the Inferno, in his *Divina Commedia*, introduces Ugolino as gnawing the skull of the archbishop Roger, and causes him to relate his feelings on hearing the gates closed and seeing his children perish.

The moment represented in the picture may be

supposed to be that in which he thus expresses himself:

" Come un poco di raggio si fumesso
   Nel doloroso carcere edis scorsi
    Per gnattro viso il mio aspetta stesso
Ambo le mani per dolor mi morsi."

When a glimmering light had entered
   The melancholy prison, and I saw
   My own in the four countenances before me,
I gnawed both my hands with grief.

He continues affectingly to relate, that his children, thinking he did this from hunger, entreat of him rather to make them suffer than to bereave them of his protection. The tower was opened eight days after they had been deprived of food, when it was found they had all perished. It was long known by the name of the " tower of hunger."

## 68.—*Duchess of Cleveland.*

Barbara, countess of Castlemaine, and afterwards duchess of Cleveland, was the daughter and heiress of William Villiers, viscount Grandison, who died in 1642, of the wounds he received at the battle of Edgehill. Some time before the Restoration, she married Roger Palmer, Esq., then a student in the Temple, and heir to a considerable fortune; and who, in the thirteenth year of the reign of Charles II, was created count Castlemaine in Ireland. She had a daughter born in 1661; shortly after which she became the acknowledged mistress of the king, who continued his connexion with her till 1672, when she was brought to bed of a daughter, supposed to be the child of Mr. Churchill, afterwards duke of Marlborough, and which the king did not acknowledge. Her gallantries were many, and not unknown to the king. In 1670, she was created baroness of Nonsuch, in the county of Surry, countess of Southampton, and duchess of Cleveland during her life, in reversion after her death to Charles or George Fitzroy, her first and third sons, and their heirs male. In July 1705, her husband died, and shortly after she married a man loaded with debts, known by the name of "handsome Fielding." His conduct towards her was so infamous that she was obliged to have recourse to the laws for protection. It was at length discovered that Fielding had a wife living, consequently the marriage was declared null. She survived this discovery two years, and died in October 1709, aged sixty-nine.

Burnet says she was " a woman of great beauty, but of little mind, very corrupt and greedy of money, proud, tormenting the king, of whom she feigned herself jealous to excess, though she herself was always engaged in intrigues. The passion of the monarch for her, and her strange conduct with respect to himself, so much disordered his mind, that he frequently was not master of himself, nor in a state to attend to his affairs, which at the time demanded great attention and application."

## 69.—*A Chinese Youth,*

Whose name is said to have been Warnoton. He came to England for improvement, and was educated at the Grammar-school of Sevenoaks. His portrait was painted for the duke of Dorset by Sir Joshua Reynolds.

## 70.—*The Coligni Family.*

These are portraits of cardinal de Coligni and his two brothers.

Odet de Coligni, cardinal of Chatillon, archbishop of Toulouse, &c., was a learned and distinguished prelate of the Roman Catholic faith; but marrying, and embracing the Protestant religion, he was stripped of the purple, and compelled to fly to England, where he was poisoned by his valet, in 1571.

Francis de Coligni was a colonel in the army, and distinguished himself in several battles, in the cause of the Calvinists. He died in 1569.

Gaspard de Coligni signalized himself in his youth, in the reigns of Francis I, and Henry II,

and was made colonel of infantry and admiral of
France, in 1552. He also embraced the reformed
religion, and his opposition to the house of Guise
was so formidable, that it was feared he would
overthrow the French government. On the
peace which followed the battles of Jarnac and
Montcontour, Charles IX. deluded him into
security by a present of 100,000 livres, and other
favours; but his fate was sealed; and though he
escaped one attempt on his life, being shot at
from a window, at the marriage of the prince
de Navarre, afterwards Henry IV, he was only
reserved as one of the victims of the brutal
massacre of St. Bartholomew's day, 1572. His
house was broken into, he was stabbed in several
places, and his body thrown out of the window,
hung by the feet on a gibbet, and exposed for
three days to the insults of a misguided mob.

## 71.—*James Butler, Duke of Ormond,*

Was born in 1610, and succeeded his grandfather
in the earldom of Ormond, in 1632. In 1641, at
the breaking out of the Irish rebellion, he was
appointed lieutenant-general of an army of three
thousand men, and succeeded in arresting the
progress of the insurgents, a service for which he
was created a marquess. In 1643, he defeated
the rebels under Preston; and was shortly after

appointed lord-lieutenant of Ireland. When the royal cause was altogether ruined, he went to France; but after the death of Charles I. returned to Ireland. Here, however, his efforts to rouse the people were unavailing; and when Cromwell landed, the marquess re-embarked for France. At the restoration, he was raised to an Irish dukedom, and appointed lord-lieutenant of Ireland; but, for his attachment to lord Clarendon, incurred the displeasure of the court, and was deprived of his office. In 1670, the infamous colonel Blood, whom he had imprisoned in Ireland, attempted to seize his person, and hang him at Tyburn. He was for this purpose actually taken out of his carriage, gagged, and placed behind a powerful horseman; but the duke, by his personal exertions, threw himself and the villain off the horse, and obtained assistance. At the desire of the king, he afterwards consented to forgive Blood, saying, " that if his majesty could pardon him for attempting to steal the crown, he might easily do so for an attempt upon his life." He was at length again appointed to the vice-royalty of Ireland, and in 1682 advanced to an English dukedom. He died at Kingston Hall, in Dorsetshire, in 1688, and was buried in Westminster abbey.

THE END.

# LIST OF SUBSCRIBERS.

———◆———

AMHERST, the Right Hon. Earl; 3 copies, LARGE PAPER.

Amherst, Lady Sarah.

Auber, Rev. R. H., Shoreham; 2 copies, 1 L. P.

Austen, Rev. J., Chevening.

Alexander, Thomas, esq., Edenbridge.

Ashdowne, Miss, Tunbridge; L. P.

Atkins, J. P., esq., Halsted Place; 2 copies, 1 L. P.

Austen, G. L., esq.

Austen, Mrs. G. L.

Austen, Mrs. Col., Kippington; L P.

Adams, Mr.

Allwork, Mr.

Anquetil, Mr.; 2 copies.

Arrow, Mr.; L. P.

Atherfold, Mr. John, Westerham.

2 K 2

Bayley, Sir John.

Bailey, Rev. R. R., rector of the Tower, London.

Board, Rev. R., Westerham ; L. P.

Briggs, Rev. J., Bessel's-green.

Britten, Rev.

Bailey, Captain James A.

Boraston, Mrs. G. B., Wendron, Cornwall.

Bosworth, Thomas H., esq., Westerham.

Buckley, H., esq., Riverhill.

Butler, Mrs., Tunbridge Wells; 2 copies, 1 L. P.

Bain, Mrs.

Barham, Mr., Chipsted.

Biggs, Mr., Ightham.

Blake, Mr. T., London.

Bligh, Mr. S.

Booth, Mr., Sundridge.

Bowles, Mr. R., Shoreham.

Bowra, Mr.

Briggs, Mr.

Bryant, Mr. J. B., Westerham.

Budd, Mrs., King-street, Maidstone.

Burgess, Mrs., Kemsing.


Camden, the Most Noble the Marquess, Wildernesse Park; L. P.

Cobb, Rev. S. W.; Ightham L. P.

Connell, Rev. James, Lympsfield.

Cornish, Rev. A., Chevening.

Curteis, Rev. T.; L. P.

Cade, Mrs., Riverhead; L. P.

Carnell, T., esq.

Clark, Miss; 2 copies.

Cole, G. C., esq.; L. P.

Cooke, Mrs., Marina, St. Leonard's.

Cooke, Miss......ditto.

Crow, Mrs. R., Ightham.

Campart, Mr.

Carrington, Mr. O.; 2 copies.

Clark, Mrs.

Colbran, Mr. J., Tunbridge Wells.

Colgate, Mr. H., Chevening.

Corke, Mr. S.

Covell, Mr. G.

Covell, Mr. J.

Cramer & Co. Messrs., London.

Creasy, Mr. William, Edenbridge.


Delawarr, Countess of, Buckhurst; 2 copies, L. P.

D'Oyly, Rev. Dr., Sundridge, L. P.

Dalton, Mr. George, Westerham.

Davis, Mr. N., Westerham.

Deane, Mr.

Doggett, Mr., Old Buckhurst.

Duncan, Mr. John, Westerham.


Edwards, Mr.

Edwards, Miss.

Fowler, Mr. R., Gabriel's-hill, Maidstone.
Franks, Mr. G.
Frederick, Miss ; 2 copies.

Grasett, W., esq, Ovenden ; L. P.
George, Mr. Henry, Westerham ; 1 L. P. and 6
  SM. P.
Gibbon, Mr. T.
Gosling, Mr., Bessel's-green.
Green, Miss.
Green, Mr. Thomas, Westerham.

Holmesdale, Lord, Montreal.
Harward, Rev. J. Netherton, Oak Bank ; L. P.
Hasted, Rev. E., Hollingbourne ; L. P.
Heath, Mr. W. H. W., Tunbridge ; L. P.
Heawood, Rev. E., Halsted.
Hecker, Rev. H. T.
Harman, Mrs. T., Tunbridge ; L. P.
Hughes, H., esq., Bradbourne ; 2 copies.
Harding, Miss, Rusthall.
Harman, Miss, Calverley Lodge, Tunbridge
  Wells ; L. P.
Haslop, Mrs., Buckhurst.
Hayton, Mrs., Edenbridge.
Howard, Mr. John, Westerham.
Hoate, Mr., Wythyham.
Hodson, Mr. J., Reading.
How, Mr. G.

Hubbard, Mr., Sundridge.

Jowett, Rev. —, Hartfield.
James, Mrs. G., Court Lodge, Ightham ; 2 copies.
Johnson, Mr. S. B., Heysden.
Jones, Mr. ; 2 copies.

Kidder, Mrs., Westerham.

Lacy, Mrs.
Love, Mrs., Filstone.
Love, Miss J., ditto ; L. P.
Leake, Mrs. Martin, Woodhurst, Oxted ; L. P.
Lewis, F. W., esq., Westerham.
Loveday, Mrs., Westerham.
Lucas, Mr.
Luckhurst, Mr.
Luckhurst, Mr. D., Tunbridge.

Macleod, Mrs., Riverhead ; L. P.
Master, C. L. H., esq., Barrow-Green House,
    Oxted ; L. P.
Mayers, J. P., esq., Brasted ; L. P.
Minet, C. W., esq., Hever's-Wood, Brasted.
Monson, W. J., esq., Chart Lodge, Seal ; L. P.
Morland, Miss ; L. P.
Morris, R. W. G., esq. ; L. P.
Mount, W. F., esq., Riverhead ; L. P.
Mount, Mrs. .... ...ditto ; L. P.
Martyr, Miss, Bessel's-green.

Marlborough, Mr., London.
Martin, Mr., Chipsted.
Martin, Mr. H.; Foot's Cray.
Mechanics' Institution. Westerham.
Morphew, Mrs.; L. P.

Nepean, Captain Evan, Bradbourne Vale; L. P.
Nash, Mr. E., Otford.
Noakes, Mr. James, Westerham.

Onslow, Rev. M. Weald.
Owen, Mr., London.

Plymouth, the Right Hon. Countess-Dowager of;
    3 copies, L. P.
Pratt, Lady G., Wildernesse Park, Seal; L. P.
Peete, Rev. W. W., Chelsfield; L. P.
Plucknett, Rev. W., Sundridge
Price, Rev. R., Shoreham
Payne, Mrs. E., Swalcliffe, Oxon.
Pearson, John, esq., Tandridge Hall.
Petley, Mrs.; L. P.
Petley, C. R. C., esq., Riverhead; 3 copies, L. P.
Petley, Mr. H.; L. P.
Polhill, George, esq., Sundridge; L. P.
Palmer, Mr. Thomas, East Grinstead.
Palmer, Mr. Joseph; 2 copies.
Parker, Mr. T.
Payne, Mr., sen., London.

Payne, Mr. W., London.
Payne, Mr. John.
Payne, Mr., Bolebrook.
Pawson, Mr. S.
Pawson, Mr. J. ; 3 copies.
Penny, Mr., London ; 2 copies.

Rycroft, Sir Richard, Everlands ; L. P.
Reed, Mr.

Streatfeild, Rev. Thomas, Chart's Edge, Wester-
   ham ; L. P.
Sutcliffe, Rev. J., Knockholt
Sale, Miss, Westerham.
Selby, T., esq., Ightham ; L. P.
Streatfeild, Miss B. E., Westerham.
Sturley, Miss ; L. P.
Salt, Mr. T. P., London.
Sanders, Mr. ; 2 copies.
Seale, Mr. J.
Seale, Miss C.
Seale, Miss E.
Sharp, Mr., Riverhead.
Shewen, Mrs., sen.
Shewen, Mr.
Slee, Mr. N., London.
Smith, Miss.
Southern, Mr. T.
Summerfield, Miss.

Taylor, Mr. J. Seal.
Thompson, C. M., esq., Westerham.
Thompson, Mr. Thomas, Westerham.
Thorpe, Miss, Greatness.
Turner, Mr. Summerford.

Wallace, Rev. J. L.
Wilgress, Rev. J. T., Riverhead.
Wood, Rev. W., Farnborough; L. P.
Wallis, —, esq., Hartfield.
Whittaker, Mrs. Mariners, Westerham.
Willard, C., esq.; L. P.
Willard, Miss, Westerham, L. P.
Willmott, C., esq., Sundridge; L. P,
Wilson, Mr., Buckhurst.
Winn, Mr. C.

PAYNE, PRINTER, SEVENOAKS.

*Announcement by the Author of this Volume.*

IN THE PRESS,

AND SPEEDILY WILL BE PUBLISHED IN QUARTO,

*Price Two Guineas,*

THE

# HERALDRY OF KENT,

CONTAINING

## The Full Armorial Bearings of the Nobility and Gentry,

*Being Resident-Natives of that County,*

PROPERLY BLAZONED, AND ENGRAVED WITH ACCURACY AND ELEGANCE,

With the Origin of their Arms and Crests, whenever possible, their Mottos, and Biographical Notices of Distinguished Persons.

## BY JOHN H. BRADY, F.R.A.S. &c.

### CONDITIONS OF PUBLICATION.

The price to Subscribers to be *Two Guineas* in cloth boards, which will in many cases be little more than the expense of engraving their arms : not to be paid until the work be delivered.

The work will be printed on a superior paper, and in a good type; and the Engravings executed by an artist of well-known experience in heraldic illustrations.

\*\*\* *All Communications are to be addressed to the Author, at his residence, No. 10, Great College Street, Camden Town; or to the care of the Publishers,*

MESSRS. LONGMAN, ORME, BROWN, GREEN, AND LONGMANS, LONDON;

By whom also Subscribers' Names will be received.

**STAMP OFFICE,**

**AND CIRCULATING LIBRARY.**

---

# J. PAYNE,

## Stationer, Printer, Boockseller and Binder,

**SEVENOAKS,**

Has constantly on Sale a good assortment of

**Bibles, Prayer Books, &c. in plain and elegant Bindings,**

**WRITING PAPERS, ACCOUNT BOOKS,**

*PALMER'S PORTABLE PENS,*

**CARDS, CARD CASES, AND POCKET BOOKS,**

**DRAWING MATERIALS,**

**MUSIC AND MUSIC BOOKS,**

ALBUMS, SKETCH BOOKS, AND BLOTTING CASES,

**PORCELAIN AND IVORY TABLETS,**

*TUNBRIDGE WARE,*

BERLIN PATTERNS, CANVAS AND WOOL,

**PURSE SILK,**

**BAG-TASSELS, AND CORD,**

**TOILET AND SMELLING BOTTLES,**

**Perfumery,**

**BEST STEEL SCISSARS AND PENKNIVES,**

**TORTOISESHELL COMBS,**

HAIR, NAIL, TOOTH, AND CLOTHES BRUSHES,

**DRESSING CASES, &c.**

CPSIA information can be obtained at www.ICGtesting.com
Printed in the USA
LVOW03s1534310515

440604LV00013B/376/P